D1636870

TRIALS OF
BRIAN DONALD HUME

CELEBRATED TRIALS SERIES
GENERAL EDITOR: JONATHAN GOODMAN

This book is dedicated
to
HIS HONOUR JUDGE ELAM

CELEBRATED TRIALS

TRIALS OF BRIAN DONALD HUME

With an Introduction
and Edited by

IVAN BUTLER

DAVID & CHARLES
NEWTON ABBOT   LONDON
NORTH POMFRET (VT)   VANCOUVER

ISBN 0 7153 7118 5

Library of Congress Catalog Card Number 76–4366

Set in 11 on 12pt Linotype Baskerville and printed in
Great Britain by Latimer Trend & Company Ltd Plymouth
for David & Charles (Publishers) Limited
Brunel House   Newton Abbot   Devon

Published in the United States of America
by David & Charles Inc
North Pomfret   Vermont 05053   USA

Published in Canada
by Douglas David & Charles Limited
1875 Welch Street   North Vancouver   BC

CONTENTS

THE TRIAL
First Day

Evidence for the Prosecution

Second Day

5

The plan of Hume's flat was kindly supplied by Syndication International

EDITOR'S NOTE

I should like to express my sincere thanks to the following: His Honour Judge Elam; Sir Norman Skelhorn, Mr T. J. Taylor and the office of the Director of Public Prosecutions, for making various records available to me; the *Sunday Mirror,* for permission to make use of Brian Donald Hume's two 'Confessions', published in the *Sunday Pictorial;* Mr John Williams, for permission to quote from his book, *Hume —Portrait of a Double Murderer;* Dame Rebecca West, for permission to quote from her essay on Hume in her book, *A Train of Powder,* and a long personal letter on the case; ex-Deputy Commander Colin MacDougall and Mr F. Donal Barry, CBE, for sparing time to talk to me about Hume; Mr Basil Donne-Smith and Mr James Fitzgerald, for help in obtaining out-of-print material; Mr Robert Broeder, for assistance with the illustrations; finally, Mr Jonathan Goodman, the Series Editor, for his help.

On 20 August, 1976, just before this book was passed for press, Brian Donald Hume was flown back from Switzerland, after sixteen years in prison, and, after examination at Heathrow Airport by two doctors, taken to Broadmoor.

INTRODUCTION

1949 was a grey, drab year in a grey, drab world. The miserable aftermath of war reached its lowest point of depression. The dreary shortages of those small luxuries that help to make life tolerable dragged interminably on. The cities were pitted with bomb sites and scarred with blitzed buildings. The expectations of a 'better world' deliberately instilled into the people to keep them up to the fighting mark were being more and more clearly revealed as the false hopes they were. It was a year of tired disillusionment, of chaos and trickery, accurately and unforgettably preserved (even though the setting was Vienna in defeat rather than London in victory) in the masterly film by Graham Greene and Carol Reed, *The Third Man*.

Spivs and wide boys, black-marketeering, under-the-counter dealing—it all formed a fitting breeding-place and background for the activities, and the ultimate crimes, of Brian Donald Hume.

'I was born,' said Hume, in the 'Confession' given to the *Sunday Pictorial* and published during June 1958, 'with a chip on my shoulder, large as an elephant. I've got a grudge against society,'* Whatever lies he may have told on other occasions, there is little doubt that here, at any rate, he was speaking the truth. He laid the blame for this grudge on the fact that all his life he had had to fight 'the shame and degradation of not knowing who my father was'.

His birthplace was at Swanage, Dorset. Born in December 1919, he was the illegitimate son of a schoolmistress, the sister of a well-known scientist. The circumstances were kept secret from him, and he was told by his mother to call her 'Aunt Doodie'. At the age of about three he was sent to an institution at Burnham-on-Sea, in Somerset. The place was run by three

*Unless otherwise stated, all direct quotations from Hume in this Introduction are from the 'Confession'.

ladies and seems—if his account is to be believed—to have been a grim home indeed. The small inmates were beaten, badly fed, made to sleep in scandalously overcrowded and insanitary conditions, teased and tormented at the whim of the staff. On one occasion a member of the staff dressed up as an old gypsy to play a particularly mean and frightening trick on a small girl and himself. Hume saw through her disguise and violently attacked her. As John Williams states in his book on Hume'* this incident must have been of prime psychological importance in his development. The 'gypsy' had been used as a means of terrifying the children for a long time. In an outburst of raging fury (he actually chased his tormentor, brandishing a chopper) he was able to assert himself and overcome his fear.

At the age of eight he was unexpectedly removed from these unappetising surroundings and taken into the care of his grandmother, a kindly woman who lived in Hendon, not far from the spot where he was later to commit the first of his murders. There, apparently, he was settling down fairly happily, making friends with other boys in the London streets, and discovering a love for the cinema—particularly crime films. After only a few months, however, he was moved once again and sent to his 'Aunt Doodie', who was now married to a motor engineer and living near Basingstoke; she was head-mistress of a village school. Though treated kindly enough, he seems never to have felt at home with his 'aunt' and her family: he longed to be back with his grandmother, and was shattered when, a few months later, she died. But a far worse shock awaited him. One day, after he had been puzzled for some while by odd remarks made to him by other children, he was informed by a servant in the house that the woman he had been told to look on as his aunt was in reality his mother. It was a shattering discovery, and though it appeared that she was acting from the kindest of motives in having him back to live with her, he developed a deep and ineradicable hatred towards her. The death of his grandmother—the one person from whom, according to his own account, he had received anything like affection during these formative years—had already strengthened his general bitterness, and he felt

*Hume—Portrait of a Double Murderer, Heinemann, 1960.

increasingly frustrated and insecure, an outsider in his own home.

At length he performed a symbolic act of revenge. His mother owned a pedigree cockerel which, he said, used to charge him when he went to feed the poultry. 'One day I took my mother's small-bore gun and shot the cockerel. Then I threw the cockerel into the cesspool and pretended it had drowned. Nineteen years later, as I flew across the Channel to dispose of the cut-up body of Stanley Setty, I remembered that cockerel.'

Far from unintelligent, he passed the entrance examination to the local grammar school in 1931, and won a scholarship that might have given him a good chance of entering a university. Two years later he was removed from school (reported as 'not satisfactory') and, after working as a house-boy near Farnborough for a few months, he ran away from the place he had never regarded as home, and made his way to London. After spending a night sleeping rough on Barnes Common, he went to Somerset House, and there uncovered the secret—and proved the truth—of his birth: where the name of his father should have been there was a blank space.

He returned to Barnes Common for his suitcases which he had left under a bush, and then thumbed a lift from a lorry into London. Though he neither knew nor cared where he was going, this could in fact have been a turning-point in his life. Through the good offices of the lorry-driver, a builder, he met the woman who above all others might have softened some of the bitterness and hatred that festered in him. She was a Mrs Clare, wife of the builder's foreman, who took Hume into her home in Paddington as a lodger. She looked after him and mothered him, but there is no mention of her in the 'Confession'. At fifteen he obtained a job as an apprentice electrician, earning twenty-five shillings a week, then wrote a harsh letter to his mother ('vomiting the vindictiveness of my soul in words'), saying he never wished to see her again. The final severance from his mother, and the friendship of Mrs Clare, might have been the start of a fresh and brighter existence, but allied to his grudge against society was an over-riding ambition to make money—by any means. 'I was after the big cash to help me do all the things that had been denied to me.' He embarked almost immediately on a career of petty thieving; joining a gang of hooligans in the Paddington and Hammersmith areas, he stole cars for joy-rides and generally disturbed the peace.

At seventeen he joined the Communist Party—more as a personal gesture of defiance than from any deep political convictions. He himself gave as his reason: 'because I thought I could get something for nothing'. He sold the *Daily Worker* in the West End streets, and participated with apparent relish in the Fascist/Communist clashes of the late nineteen-thirties. At about the same time he developed a passion for aeroplanes. When he was working on the wiring of a new house, says Rebecca West,* 'he could always tell where he had been, because he had scribbled drawings of aircraft on the plastered walls.' When the Spanish Civil War broke out, he tried to join the International Brigade but was turned down on account of his youth.

In 1939 he joined the RAF Volunteer Reserve, giving his occupation as a fitter; at the outbreak of war he enlisted in the Royal Air Force. After three weeks at Uxbridge and Debden, he was posted to the Initial Training Wing at Hastings.

Unfortunately, his service career was soon cut short. In 1940 he was badly injured in an accident while on a night practice flight at Andover. According to his own account, he mistook the lights of a grounded plane for those of the runway and crashed on top of it. The crew of the plane were killed, and Hume suffered severe head injuries. Following this he had an attack of cerebro-spinal meningitis, and was declared unfit for duty. After a spell as a member of the ground staff, he was found to be unfit for this also, and was discharged; he had been in the service about eighteen months.

During his illness a highly significant psychological report was issued on his general condition: 'Having suffered from meningitis, he has developed a degree of organically determined psychopathy, as a result of which his mentality, particularly as evinced by his political opinions, has lost its plasticity, thereby rendering permanent what might have been an other-

*In 'Mr Setty and Mr Hume', a long and exceedingly interesting essay on the case, included in her book *A Train of Powder* (Macmillan, 1955).

wise purely transient adolescent phase in the social maturation
of a "Bolshie".'

He took a job as fire-spotter, and tried unsuccessfully to get
back into the RAF. At the same time a change in his domestic
circumstances aggravated his bolshieness. Mrs Clare's daughter
and her husband, together with their baby, were bombed out,
and Mrs Clare took them into her own house. This roused
Hume's jealousy to an unnatural and eventually an intoler-
able degree; before long, he was making such a nuisance of
himself that Mrs Clare had to ask him to leave. It was a tragic
conclusion to a generous attempt on the part of a stranger
to give him help and a chance to make something of his life.
'Now,' he says in the 'Confession', 'I launched myself into a
life of spivery that was to lead me to Stanley Setty.'

He turned his fire-spotting chore at the Napier engineering
works in Acton to personal advantage by giving false raid
alarms and then, while everyone else was sheltering, pilfering
tinned food and other items from the canteen to sell in the
black market. He also conceived the idea of manufacturing
gin from surgical spirit and selling the resulting concoction to
night clubs. This proved to be quite a successful venture,
bringing him in about £60 a week, until the firm from which
he was obtaining (by fraudulent means) his supply of surgical
spirit discovered what was happening and put a swift stop to
it.

At some point during this period he met an IRA member,
who sold him a couple of guns. 'I had no ammunition with
them,' he said; 'they just made me feel good.' He did not feel
quite so good, however, when he was met and searched at the
factory gate by two police officers; he considered himself
fortunate in not having the guns on him that particular afternoon. It turned out that in fact the police were interested in
him from another angle—as a possible spy. The firm where
he was fire-watching had been working on a top-secret power
plant, and Hume had been observed with a photograph. This
was, at the time, strictly forbidden; he was taken to Scotland
Yard and questioned, then released with a caution.

Shortly afterwards he acquired an RAF officer's uniform,
complete with wings (purchasing the lot for £5), and an RAF
identity card. With these he toured the country from airfield

to airfield, posing as a Battle of Britain hero, accepting the hospitality of the mess, and passing dud cheques. This led eventually to a more serious confrontation with the authorities. By June 1942 the imposture had been discovered, and he was arrested when cashing a cheque for £25 at Northolt airport. By chance, the two police officers who interviewed him were the same men who had been in charge of the investigation into the affair of the suspicious photograph. This time there was more than suspicion. Hume found himself in the dock at the Old Bailey, and was remanded for a month to Feltham Borstal in order to undergo a medical examination. While there—probably feeling somewhat sorry for himself—he wrote to Mrs Clare. She responded with kindness and food parcels, but once he was free he apparently had no further use for her and it seems he never contacted her again.

Back at the Old Bailey, he came before the Recorder, Sir Gerald Dodson, who bound him over for two years—letting him off, it might be thought, extremely lightly. 'I was still under twenty-one,' he said, 'an undesirable and unreliable character.'*

However, this second brush with the law seems to have struck a warning note which he heeded to some extent—for a time. He took a course at the British School of Radio Telegraphy, qualified as a radio engineer, and started out on his own in the electrical business. Making more or less legal use of his intelligence for the first time paid reasonably handsome dividends. As a sideline he worked as a plumber (apparently with no qualifications whatsoever except a knack of profiting from an ability to pick up knowledge from hit-or-miss experience), cheating his customers whenever it was safe to do so. After a period of doing random repair and installation jobs he had made enough money by early 1943 to open his own radio and electrical shop, the Hume Electric Co Ltd, taking premises at 620 Finchley Road, Golders Green. In those days of shortage and scarcity, aggravated later by the damage caused by the V1 and V2 weapons, the demand for such work was considerable, and Hume flourished as a result. In addition to his routine work, he designed and manufactured his own 'Little Atom' toaster (of which he sold 50,000), an electric

---

*In fact, he must have been twenty-two or twenty-three.

towel rail, and a mechanical toy. By the end of 1944 he was making something like £100 a week profit, and by 1947 was employing a considerable staff and had acquired extra premises, two vans and a luxury car. Around this time he also bought a dog—a half-husky, half-Alsatian called Tony—who was to play some small part in the events that followed.

Two years after the war, then, it seemed that Brian Donald Hume could look forward to a reasonably prosperous business career. One night in 1947 he went into the bar of the 'M' Club in Welbeck Street and there met a man named Renato Kahn and his wife, Cynthia. Hume was at once attracted to the woman, and in September 1948, after her divorce from Kahn, he married her. (A press report at the time of the trial in 1950 gave the meeting-place of Hume and his future wife as Hay-on-Wye, where her parents lived, but this appears to be an error.) A vivid picture of Cynthia Hume—one of the most interesting characters in the not very inspiring cast of the Hume drama—is given by Rebecca West, writing not long after the trial.

> Cynthia Hume had an unusual and very strong personality. She was twenty-nine, and looked six or seven years younger. She had soft, dark hair, gentle eyes, a finely cut and very childish mouth, and an exceptionally beautiful creamy complexion. Her fault was that she appeared colourless . . . In compensation she had a low-pitched and very lovely voice and a charm that, had she been a mermaid, would have drawn all navies down into deep water, man by man . . . She was not intellectual, but she was shrewd. Perhaps she was too languid to use her shrewdness to avert catastrophe; but she could survive catastrophe.*

Brought up in comfortable surroundings and well educated, Cynthia Hume was the daughter of a chief examiner in a midland savings bank. Her first marriage, an unhappy one, introduced her to the night life of London's West End (according to Hume she 'wanted the gay life'), and when he met her she was secretary in a fashionable restaurant.

Towards the end of 1947, Hume had another encounter. He required a cheap car for one of his staff, and outside a café in Warren Street—then a sort of *al fresco* car mart—he was

*Rebecca West, op cit.

introduced to, and haggled with, a dealer, eventually completing the transaction. He noted that the man—swarthy, fourteen stone in weight, about forty-four years old—had 'a voice like broken bottles, and pockets stuffed with cash'. His name, to which Hume probably gave but passing attention, was Stanley Setty.

Around this time, Hume's business began to suffer from the post-war pinch, and orders slackened off; the situation was not helped by his paying too much attention to Cynthia and not enough to the business. One day he visited her parents' home in Kington, Herefordshire. Her father told him that there was a small factory to be had in Castle Street in nearby Hay-on-Wye, which might suit him better than London. The idea appealed to Hume. He sold the lease of the Finchley Road shop, retaining the upper maisonette, and began an attempt to rebuild his fortunes in the country, naming the business Little Atom Electrical Products. Hay, a small country town of some character, had a congruous association with Hume as the place where the poisoner Major Armstrong had his offices; and an incongruous one as a place frequently visited and referred to by that most enchanting of Victorian diarists, the Reverend Francis Kilvert. It must have been a lively place during Hume's brief sojourn, for he had turned his inventive mind towards the manufacture of fireworks (to be called Hume Bangers). The resulting experiments blew out the windows of the factory, and the place was subsequently damaged in two fires.

Early in 1949 Hume returned to Finchley Road, where Cynthia had remained during the period he was in Herefordshire. Business and funds continued to dwindle, and the future looked bleak. In order to recover the wealth that had once been his but was his no longer, Hume decided to become a 'super-spiv'. 'On the creep for a shady deal', he drifted into the Hollywood Club, near Marble Arch. It was a fatal drift. Propped against the bar was the car dealer he had casually met some months before.

Stanley Setty's real name was Sulman Seti. He was born in Baghdad in 1903 and brought to England at four years of age, when his name was anglicised. The family settled in Manchester, and at fourteen young Stanley began working in a cotton-mill. But he did not stay long at the looms. When he was only sixteen, he set up as a shipping merchant with his brother. Their capital was a little under £2,000. After two years, the youthful firm had assets of £5 against debts of something like £15,000. A receiving order was granted (Stanley being still too young to be made a bankrupt), and the enterprising venture came to grief. In 1926 he started up again, dealing in a variety of merchandise. His business methods somewhat resembling those of his future murderer, he was sentenced in 1928 to eighteen months' imprisonment for numerous offences against the bankruptcy acts. For the next ten years he led a drab, hand-to-mouth existence, earning a few pounds a week as a dealer on commission; but the war, with its black markets and shortages, proved for Setty, as for Hume, a godsend. By 1947 he was dealing busily, if none too scrupulously, in second-hand cars, running a garage in Cambridge Terrace Mews by Regent's Park. Few questions were asked as to where the cars came from, or why it was that they appeared to be so handily obtainable in those difficult times from the obliging Mr Setty. Customers were presumably satisfied, and so was he: big money was coming his way. Even this none-too-immaculate occupation, however, was merely a front for other activities, such as gun-running in the Middle East, and petrol-coupon forgeries nearer home.

For Hume, the encounter with such a man was the meeting of twin minds. 'We soon realised,' he said succinctly and not surprisingly, 'that we could be useful to each other.' Their first transaction was a modest one—the sale by Hume of a gross of American nylon stockings at £1 per pair, with promises of bigger deals to come but only a fortnight later Hume committed himself finally to the shady world of his broken-bottle-voiced acquaintance by joining in the petrol-coupon racket. Car deals followed. Hume 'snatched' six cars, two of them Jaguars, received £300 a time from Setty, and was back in the money again.

Of importance to the events that followed was another of Setty's sideline occupations, that of a kerbside banker: a casher of cheques who would, for a discount, pay ready money,

B

no questions asked, and then pass the cheque on to an associate who had a banking account. This was a much appreciated service to anyone who had an illegal transaction to cover up, or a tax to evade; it meant that a cheque could be converted into cash without any direct record remaining. It also meant that Setty usually had, and was known to have, large sums of money on his person.

Encouraged and enriched by his new contacts, Hume also started to develop interests of his own. His love of flying had never abated and therefore, combining business with pleasure, he took up air smuggling, after joining the United Services Flying Club at Elstree in Hertfordshire and qualifying for a licence which enabled him to fly solo. There was at the time a fairly steady demand for this rather novel form of smuggling, and Hume was eminently suited to take advantage of it. Much of the traffic was in arms for the Near East—Israeli and Arab being served alike and indiscriminately. Hume became so proficient that he was known as The Flying Smuggler—a title one can imagine bringing him considerable satisfaction. His links with Setty strengthened, and not only on business levels. They were soon meeting socially, and Setty often went along with Hume to the maisonette for a chat. According to Hume, he took Cynthia to meet Setty at a night-club and noticed that his associate 'appeared most impressed with her'.

Number 620 Finchley Road, which for some years now has housed a greengrocer's shop on the ground floor, is a few yards from the busy centre dominated by Golders Green Station. A few houses beyond the shop in the other direction stood the little Ionic Cinema, a building of some historic interest in its class, but now demolished. The house itself is a fairly typical example of commercial suburban building at the turn of the century. Though it appears roomy from the outside, and contains two separate dwellings apart from the shop, the accommodation is limited. Hume's maisonette consisted of the two top floors. Rebecca West, who visited it at the time of the trial, describes it as follows:

A dark, steep and narrow staircase with a murderous turn to it led past the front door of the lower maisonette, which was inhabited by a schoolmaster and his wife, up to Hume's own front door, which opened on a slit of a lobby. To the left was a living-room, looking over the street; to the right was a smaller dining-room, long and narrow, with beyond it a pantry, and beyond that again an attic kitchenette, with the slant of the roof coming fairly low. None of these rooms was large. The living-room was, perhaps, fifteen feet by eleven, and the dining-room fifteen feet by eight. Another steep and narrow and perilous stairway led up to a bedroom, a nursery and a bathroom . . . If anybody shouted or screamed in any room in this apartment, or if anything heavy fell on the floor, it would have been audible in all the other rooms, and almost certainly in the apartment below, and probably in the houses to the right or the left.*

This was the house to which Hume had returned to settle down with his wife and the baby girl born to her early in July 1949—the house to which Setty came for his chats with his partner about shady business deals.

Despite such mild social convivialities, however, and despite their close association in dubious practices, there was little love lost between Setty and Hume. With undoubted good reason, neither trusted the other. Spivery makes strange bedfellows, and there was a mutual dislike that grew and deepened—probably more on Hume's side than Setty's. The latter's air of unscrupulous self-confidence and his showy display of wealth aggravated Hume's festering envy: his grudge against the world in general found a point of focus near to home.

But before the outwardly trivial event which, according to Hume, brought matters to a head, there occurred—far from the scene of the crime-to-be—an extraordinary interlude, a brief moment of comedy before the drama. Equal to his passion for planes was Hume's passion for cars. During the summer of 1949 he decided to take a short break, and to give himself the pleasure of driving to Torquay in a luxury American car, a Cadillac. By chance, he arrived at the seaside resort during Carnival Week—wearing, according to a contemporary report, a red and gold-braided uniform. Some mishap to the Carnival Queen's coach had left her without a conveyance for the procession through the town, and Hume was asked if his gleaming Cadillac could be pressed into

*Rebecca West, op cit.

service. Doubtless relishing such an opportunity for display, he agreed, provided the car was not decorated and he was allowed to drive it himself. With the Chairman beside him, and the Queen and her two attendants in the rear seats, he drove slowly through the decorated streets to the cheers of the watching crowds. Hume was posing as a Pan-American pilot, having signed himself into the Grand Hotel as Captain D. B. Hulme (*sic*). 'I must say he was very goodnatured about it,' said the Chairman, Mr H. M. Chapman. 'The Carnival Queen and her attendants liked him very much. He used to tell us about his experiences as a pilot. He had a striking Canadian accent.' In a way it was, perhaps, his finest hour. When it was over he returned to Finchley Road and the grim deeds that lay ahead.

On an afternoon in August he met Setty at the Cambridge Mews garage. His dog, Tony, who was with him as usual, climbed into one of Setty's cars and scratched the paint. Setty gave the dog a kick. It was, said Hume, the worst thing he could possibly have done.

In the late afternoon of Tuesday, 4 October, 1949, Stanley Setty planned to go to Watford on business. He telephoned a friend, Miss Connie Palfreyman, to say he could not meet her that evening as arranged. At about ten minutes to six he was seen by a cousin in Great Portland Street. He was never seen alive again, except by his killer. At the time of his disappearance he was forty-six years of age, weighed some thirteen stone, and was described as wearing a blue suit with pin stripes, a cream silk shirt with flower-pattern tie, green socks and brown shoes—a somewhat distinctive outfit. In his pockets was a sum of about £1,000 in £5 notes.

Setty lived in a flat at Maitland Court, Lancaster Gate, which he shared with his sister, Mrs Ouri, and her husband. When he did not return home as usual on that Tuesday night, Mrs Ouri informed the police. His movements during that day were traced as far as possible and showed nothing out of the ordinary—business deals on the Warren Street pavement, lunch at a local restaurant. During the afternoon he had told his brother-in-law about the proposed trip to Watford.

The following afternoon his Citroën car was noticed standing near his garage in the mews. This was odd, because he usually took care to put it away. People in the mews said later that they had heard the car being parked—by Setty or somebody else—late the preceding night. Anxiety as to his whereabouts grew stronger. The family offered £1,000 for information leading to his discovery. Another sister, Mrs Sadie Spectreman, arrived from the provinces in search of news. Meanwhile, Miss Palfreyman told reporters that, while no date had been fixed for a wedding, it was hoped it would not be too far ahead—an item of news that was apparently a surprise to Setty's friends.

There was an odd occurrence three days after the disappearance. Mr and Mrs Ouri went out for the afternoon and left their front door securely fastened by two mortice locks. On their return they found the door swinging wide open. The police were called in, but found no indication that the apartment had been forcibly entered. It seemed possible that Mr Setty had come to no harm, had left home for his own purposes, and had perhaps returned briefly for some unexpected reason that afternoon. Nevertheless the search went on. Superintendent Cherrill, the Scotland Yard fingerprint expert, compared prints from the car door and steering-wheel with those of the missing man. Inquiries were made in Watford but led nowhere. The numerous bombed buildings and open spaces in London were searched, and this activity was extended to other places in the country. The knowledge that he had had so large a sum of money on him when he disappeared increased speculation that he had been murdered for the purposes of robbery. The police were informed by Miss Palfreyman that he had indeed been threatened by two men a few weeks previously.

While all this activity was taking place, Hume went about his daily business unmoved and, at first, unalarmed. 'I lay in bed, not unduly fearful, although the headlines read ALL NIGHT YARD PROBE INTO SETTY MYSTERY, and UNKNOWN VISITS TO FIVER-MAN'S FLAT.' His calm must surely have been slightly ruffled, however, on learning that Scotland Yard had issued the numbers of the £5 notes which Setty had had on him when he disappeared.

Then, on 21 October, the first part of the mystery was solved. Sidney Tiffin, a farm labourer of Tillingham, Essex, who was taking a week's holiday at home, went wild-fowling in the Dengie Marshes, a desolate stretch of mud, grasses and little rivulets down the rivers Crouch and Blackwater, about ten miles north of the Thames Estuary. There he saw a bundle floating in the water. At first he thought little about it—it might have been a drogue chute from one of the RAF training planes which frequented the district. Half-an-hour later, considering that it might be worth the trouble of reclaiming the object in order to earn the five shillings offered by the RAF for recovery, he went back to it, and found that in fact it was a package covered with felt and secured with rope. On cutting open the covering, he saw a human torso, legless and headless, in shirt and pants, the hands tied together with a leather strap. Horrified, he fastened the parcel to a stake and ran off to inform the police. By the time they arrived it was dark, so little further was done until the next morning, when the torso was taken to the mortuary at Chelmsford. There Dr Francis Camps examined it in detail. He found five stab wounds and a number of post-mortem injuries, including multiple rib fractures and fracture of the sacrum (the flat triangular bone at the base of the spine)—indicating that it might have been dropped from a height. It was also concluded that the head and legs had been severed after death by somebody with some knowledge of cutting up flesh.

Despite the absence of the head and the general decomposition of the torso, identification was not long delayed. This was made possible by a brilliant piece of work by Superintendent Cherrill—which, as the Defence accepted that the body was that of Stanley Setty, did not come out at the trial. The body had been in the water for so long that it was not possible for fingerprints to be taken by the usual method, so Cherrill tried what had been unsuccessfully attempted in several previous cases. He removed the skin from the fingers of each hand and, after treating them, laid the wrinkled tubes over his own fingers which were encased in rubber gloves. In this way he obtained a set of prints clear enough to be compared with those taken from Setty some years before. They matched exactly. Hume was later to regret that he had not thought to take the precaution of cutting off the hands of his victim.

On learning from Detective Superintendent Colin Mac-Dougall, who was the Scotland Yard officer in charge of the Essex inquiries, that the torso had very possibly fallen from a height, Chief Detective Inspector John Jamieson, who with methodical persistence had been searching for Setty, extended the field of his inquiries to airports. On Sunday, 22 October, the story of the finding of the torso was spread across the pages of the newspapers, and it was not long before a communication was received by the police from Elstree aerodrome. A member of the staff, William Davey, said that a member of a flying club there, a man named Hume, had hired a light plane on 5 October, put two parcels into it, and booked out to South-end. Davy remembered the episode because the man put one parcel in the back of the plane and one in the pilot's seat, removing the second parcel to the co-pilot's seat when the error was pointed out to him. One of the parcels was squarish and the other was of a bulky nature, between two and three feet long.

Hume had been following the news with growing anxiety ('I tried hard to go about my shady business in a normal manner as the murder hunt began'), but still reckoned that he had a fifty-fifty chance of dodging suspicion and arrest. That reckoning was proved false at 7.30 am on Thursday, 27 October, when he was taken from his bed by the police and escorted to Albany Street Police Station for questioning. When told they were making inquiries about Setty, Hume replied: 'Oh, I can't help you with that. I know nothing about it.' Later, however, he made a long, detailed, but wholly uncorroborated statement about three elusive characters, whom he said he knew as Mac or Max, Greenie and The Boy, and whose descriptions—had anyone considered it at the time—bore an astonishing resemblance to those of the police officers examining him. According to this statement, the three men, all hitherto unknown to him, approached Hume with a proposition and secured his agreement to drop parcels—at first two, then later a third—into the sea in order to avoid detection of a crime. At first he was given to understand they were bundles of plates used for forging petrol coupons, but later—he admitted—it occurred to him that he might be disposing of the dismembered body of Stanley Setty.

Hume's story, for all its ingenuity, did not impress the police to any great extent, and on 28 October he was taken from Albany Street to Bow Street and there charged with the murder of Setty. 'I didn't kill him,' he said. 'I am absolutely not guilty.'

After being remanded in custody at Brixton prison for three weeks, Hume appeared before the Bow Street magistrates in the middle of November, and his trial opened in Number One Court, Old Bailey, on 18 January 1950. Mr Justice Lewis presided; Mr Christmas Humphreys led for the Crown, assisted by Mr Henry Elam; Mr R. F. Levy led for the Defence, assisted by Mr C. H. Duveen. Hume entered the dock wearing a checked sports jacket, pullover and flannel trousers, 'all chosen,' says Rebecca West, 'to look raffish, which was then the uniform of the spiv, and he had the air of self-conscious impudence which is the spiv's hall-mark . . . He was brassy, but wistful.'

The trial lasted seven days. Mr Humphreys began his opening speech in quiet tones, pointing out that the evidence he was calling would be entirely circumstantial. No person would be called to say he saw Hume murder the dead man—there was no suggestion of any confession by Hume. He went on to describe the circumstances of Hume's association with Setty, emphasising that Hume had been hard up at the time the dead man had disappeared, but less so afterwards, that £5 notes which had belonged to Setty were found in Hume's possession; that Hume had admitted to the dropping of a man's torso in the sea from a plane; that his flat was heavily stained with blood; that he had lied 'as a murderer must lie'. Mr Humphreys briefly considered Hume's lengthy statement, with particular reference to the story of Mac, Greenie and The Boy. He pointed out that it was a true statement in regard to those facts about which Hume knew the police possessed the truth; but, Mr Humphreys suggested, the three men and their plot existed only in the fertile imagination of the accused.

The rest of the first day was taken up by prosecution

witnesses giving evidence as to Hume's monetary position, his flight from Elstree, his wanting to have a carpet cleaned and a knife sharpened, and his alleged attempt to provide a false alibi for the late afternoon of 4 October. The most important witness was Mrs Ethel Stride, a charwoman employed by Hume, who was in the flat on 5 October (when he was alleged to have cut up the body of the man he had murdered the previous evening) and who, as she said, was ordered by Hume on no account to disturb him in the kitchen because he was busy tidying up a cupboard in order to fill it with coal.

The second day of the trial began with an unexpected set-back. Overnight Mr Justice Lewis had been taken ill—an illness which proved to be fatal—and his place was taken by Mr Justice Sellers.

The jury was discharged and re-sworn, and Mr Humphreys rose to say that as the case would be tried on the evidence rather than on counsel's speeches he would speak only briefly for the prosecution. It was then proposed to recall the witnesses heard the previous day—but almost at once there was a dramatic interruption. Mr Levy, counsel for the Defence, complained to the Judge that Hume's solicitor had intercepted a telegram addressed to Mrs Hume by Mr Duncan Webb, a crime reporter on *The People,* which appeared to indicate that he was trying to prevent her from giving evidence for her husband. The matter was swiftly cleared up, and Mr Webb departed with his explanation accepted, and a reminder that to interfere with a witness was a Common Law mis-demeanour.

Two medical experts, Dr Henry Smith Holden and Dr F. E. Camps, gave evidence on the third day, describing the significance of the bloodstains in Hume's flat and the wounds in Setty's body. Mr Levy, cross-examining, suggested that it would have been very improbable, given the circumstances, for the killing to have been the work of one person only. Detective Superintendent Colin MacDougall followed. He said that a search had been made for the three men mentioned in the statement; though someone named Green had been located, he bore no resemblance to Hume's description.

The fourth day saw Mr Levy opening for the Defence. He suggested that there was rather a long road between the fact that Hume admitted disposing of the parcels and the conclusion that it was he who murdered and cut up the body. He suggested that there was in fact evidence for the existence of the three men, Mac, Greenie and The Boy, and that it was incredible—indeed impossible—that Hume, a smaller man and alone, could have stabbed Setty and cut him up in the flat on 4 and 5 October, with no one being aware of it.

Hume then went into the box, and for the remainder of that day and part of the next day denied all knowledge of the murder of Setty, and asserted that Mac, Greenie and The Boy had a very definite existence outside his own imagination. Mr Humphreys's cross-examination was taken at a rapid pace, and Hume (who wore an RAF tie for the occasion) frequently snapped back answers as quickly as he was asked questions. At the close of the first day, when asked why, if he were an honest man, he did not tell the police about the mysterious trio and their proposal, he replied brusquely: 'I am not saying I am one hundred per cent honest. I am saying I am a semi-honest man—but I am not a murderer.' At the end of his evidence Hume must have felt that he had given as good as he got in the witness-box; on more than one occasion the voices of both accused and prosecuting counsel were raised one against the other.

The next witness, Mrs Cynthia Hume, provided a contrast. She gave her evidence quietly but firmly—it amounted to little more than the fact that, as far as she knew, nothing out of the ordinary took place in her home during those days of 4 and 5 October. She said she had never met Setty. Any expectations of high drama or dramatic revelations were disappointed.

The tenant of the flat below, a headmaster named Alfred Spencer, bore out Mrs Hume's statement by saying he had heard nothing unusual, despite the fact that he was at home throughout the evening of the 4th, and that sounds travelled easily in the house. Mr Cyril Lee was called to say he had once lived in Cambridge Terrace Mews and had heard the names of Mac and The Boy, and had also seen a man answering to the description of Greenie. Medical evidence was given by Dr Donald Teare, the pathologist. 'Do you think it probable from these wounds,' Mr Levy asked him, 'that

Setty was killed by one single assailant?' After a supplementary
question from the Judge, Dr Teare replied: 'I think that
the absence of marks of defence upon the body renders it
more likely that he was killed by more than one person.'

On the sixth day Mr Levy produced a 'surprise' witness,
a writer who said that while in Paris he had come into contact
with two members of an arms-smuggling gang, known as Maxie
and The Boy.

Mr Levy and Mr Humphreys then made their closing
speeches for the Defence and the Crown respectively. Mr
Humphreys put three issues to the jury: (1) Are you satisfied
that Hume murdered Setty? (2) Was Setty murdered and
subsequently cut up in Hume's flat? (3) Do you doubt for one
moment that Hume knew perfectly well that he was disposing
of the murdered remains of Setty? If, he said, they were
satisfied that they could add (2) to (3)—about which there was
no doubt as he had virtually confessed to it—then could they
have any doubt whatsoever that they had the solution to (1),
ie that Hume was guilty?

Mr Justice Sellers started his summing-up the same afternoon, and continued for the whole of the following (seventh)
morning, going through the complex evidence in close detail.
The jury left the court at 12.30 pm on Tuesday, 26 January,
with a problem the solution to which surely came down to
these clear alternatives: Hume's uncorroborated and improbable story of Mac, Greenie and The Boy—against the apparent
improbability of his having managed to stab this heavily-
built man to death and cut up his body in a cramped,
inhabited building without either neighbour, charwoman, or
above all his wife, becoming aware that anything at all was
amiss. In the event, the jury were unable to upset the even
balance between the two improbabilities. They returned some
two and a half hours later to say they were unable to reach
a unanimous decision. Hume, according to a contemporary
report, looked puzzled. When Mr Justice Sellers discharged
them, and Mr Humphreys announced that there would be no
further proceedings on the murder charge, Hume smiled—as
well he might.

A Law Society official said at the time that, so far as he
knew, it was the first time a jury had disagreed on a murder

charge for almost fifty years. In 1901 William Gardiner was twice tried for the murder of Rose Harsent at Peasenhall, Suffolk. On each occasion the jury failed to agree. A *nolle prosequi* was entered, and Gardiner was released.

For Hume, however, there awaited a second indictment. He pleaded guilty to being an accessory after the fact, and was sentenced to twelve years' imprisonment. He stood rigidly to attention as the Judge passed sentence, then gave a small bow and walked down from the dock to the cells, with a warder on either side. The case was, to all appearances, closed. . . .

THE TRIAL

IN THE

CENTRAL CRIMINAL COURT, OLD BAILEY, LONDON

*Wednesday, 18 January 1950
and succeeding days*

BEFORE

MR JUSTICE LEWIS

and subsequently

MR JUSTICE SELLERS

(and a jury)

THE KING

versus

BRIAN DONALD HUME

MR CHRISTMAS HUMPHREYS and MR HENRY ELAM (instructed by the Director of Public Prosecutions) appeared for the Crown

MR R. F. LEVY and MR CLAUDE DUVEEN (instructed by Isadore Goldman & Son) appeared for the Accused

FIRST DAY

THE CLERK OF THE COURT: Brian Donald Hume, you are charged that on 4 October last you murdered Stanley Setty. How say you, are you guilty or not guilty?

THE PRISONER: Not guilty.

The jury was empanelled and sworn.

THE CLERK: Members of the jury, the prisoner at the Bar, Brian Donald Hume, is charged with the murder of Stanley Setty on 4 October last. To this indictment he has pleaded not guilty, and it is your charge to say, having heard the evidence, whether he be guilty or not.

MR HUMPHREYS *opened the case on behalf of the Crown*:

The charge is one of wilful murder. That being the charge, it is the duty of the Prosecution to prove it, and if when you have heard the whole of the evidence you are left in any reasonable doubt as to whether or not the Prosecution have proved their case, you will acquit. Only if you are satisfied that that charge has been proved will you find the accused guilty.

The evidence in this case will be almost entirely circumstantial. No person will be called to say he saw Hume murder the dead man, Mr Setty. There is no suggestion of any confession by the accused man that he murdered Setty. But you will be asked to consider a great mass of detailed evidence, and to put together those items of evidence in such a way that they prove, perhaps more cogently even than direct evidence, the charge brought against this man. Direct evidence can sometimes lie; people may, with the best will in the world, say they saw a certain thing happen; they may be wrong; but when you get a vast quantity of detailed evidence all adding up to one inevitable conclusion, you may regard that as proof.

Hume, the man you are trying, and Setty, the man it is alleged he killed, knew each other in the car markets of London in Great Portland Street and Warren Street. Hume was hard up on 4 October, when it is alleged he killed Setty. On that day Setty drew from his bank £1,005 in £5 notes. That night someone murdered Setty with five stab wounds.

Thereafter, Hume was found in possession of a quantity of
£5 notes. On his own confession, four of them corresponded
in numbers with the numbers of notes which had been
published in the press as being those which Setty had drawn
from the bank on 4 October.

Hume has confessed that, on 5 and 6 October, he dropped
the dismembered remains of a man he believed to be Setty in
two lots from an aeroplane over the sea near Southend. You
may agree with the proposition that he who disposes of the
body of a murdered man is usually the murderer. In Hume's
flat in Finchley Road was found heavy staining of blood, some
of which was in the same blood group as that of the murdered
man. It is clear, say the Prosecution, that on that day the
murdered man was cut up in that flat. You may agree with
the proposition that he who cuts up the body of a recently
murdered man is very probably the murderer.

Hume has made a long statement in his own defence. That
statement is, according to the Prosecution, partly true, but
only as to the facts which Hume at the time knew the police
knew, and therefore about which it would be folly to lie.
He has lied in it, but a murderer must lie. He must give some
explanation to account for his movements. He must draw
on fantasy and, to use a word Hume had used twice, he must
romance to avoid the consequences of his act. That is the
case for the Prosecution.

Now, who was Setty? Setty, the murdered man, was, perhaps
I may call him, a pavement car dealer in the car mart of
London in Great Portland Street and the area, and he also
had a garage in Cambridge Terrace Mews, NW1, where he
kept his Citroën car. He lived with his sister in Lancaster
Gate. On 4 October we know that he sent a friend of his to
his bank to cash a cheque; as a result of which his friend
gave him £1,005 in £5 notes. That evening of 4 October
Setty was seen at his garage at about 5.30. He left in the car
with a passenger, whom he dropped at Fitzroy Street, and
then drove off. At about 5.30 he was seen by his sister in
Osnaburg Street, and at about 5.50 pm he was seen by a
cousin in Great Portland Street, but he was never seen alive
again. He was expected home that night, but he did not
return. At 9 am on 5 October—a time when the Prosecution

say Setty was already murdered—his car was found outside his garage. There was no key. Someone therefore had driven it to the garage: someone who knew where Setty's garage was, as Hume knew, and someone who could have had access to Setty's keys, as the murderer could, by taking them from his pocket. After Setty was murdered in Hume's flat, someone had to remove the car from outside the flat to avoid attention: someone who could drive and had access to the key and knew where the car was garaged. That applies to Hume.

Hume had an account at the Midland Bank at Golders Green, and on 5 October paid in £90 in cash. At that time he was £78 overdrawn, with a permitted overdraft of £70. He thus became £12 in hand. Up to that time he had been hard up. Cheques had not been met, rent was getting a little low and pawn-tickets were later found on him. Men have been murdered for less than £1,005.

At lunch-time on 5 October two very important things happened. Hume called at a cleaner's next door to his flat and asked if they could dye a carpet from a pale to a darker green. He did not want to unroll the carpet in the shop and therefore had to be given an estimated price. At 1 pm, maybe a few minutes later, he went to a garage and asked a man to sharpen a carving-knife. Later that knife was found in the flat; it was blunted. It may be that he had already blunted it by cutting up a body, and maybe he wanted it to be sharpened for more cutting. However that may be, he was in a hurry; he wanted it so quickly that he could not wait for it to be properly stoned.

A charwoman, Mrs Stride, worked on Wednesday afternoons at the flat. It is really a maisonette. On the first floor you come up into the entrance hall, and on one side is what is described as the front sitting-room, and on the other side of the hall is the dining-room, and there is a straight run through from the door of the front sitting-room across the hall into the dining-room. Upstairs there is a bedroom, a nursery (because Hume was living with his wife and a three-months-old baby), and a bathroom. When Mrs Stride arrived on 5 October she noticed that the front-room carpet had gone, and Hume volunteered the information that it had been washed because there had been stains on it; the washing was

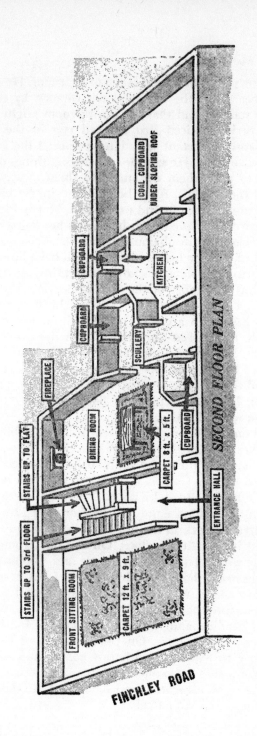

C

unsatisfactory, so it had been taken to a cleaner. He suggested that the boards on the surround not covered by the carpet should be stained, and that the dining-room might be done, too. Mrs Stride noticed that a small rug in the hall was missing. More important still, Hume wanted the kitchen to himself for an hour. He said he was tidying things out of the cupboard to pack them up and take them away. You will remember those words. After being alone in the kitchen for an hour, Hume came out and went away, Mrs Stride will say, with two parcels. Before he left he offered her half-a-crown for a new floor-cloth: quite obviously because the floor-cloth, which had vanished, was too heavily stained with fresh human blood to be shown to a charwoman, who could certainly ask questions.

Hume was a member of the United Services Flying Club at Elstree. That afternoon, 5 October, he drove with the parcels to Elstree in a car he had hired. At five o'clock he arrived. He transferred the parcels from the car to a plane and flew off. He landed an hour and a half later at Southend. There were then no parcels in the plane. Later, Hume said he dropped them in the sea. Later, he said he got a taxi back to London, leaving the plane at Southend. So much for 5 October—a well-filled day.

At 9 am on 6 October, Hume went in another hired car to Elstree, where he transferred more parcels to the waiting car which he had left there the night before. He seemed in a hurry to get back to Golders Green, and was back in Golders Green or Finchley Road by noon. There he saw a painter, a man named Staddon employed by Saunders Ltd. Staddon was prepared to work in his lunch hour for Hume, and had been called in to stain the floor. On this day Hume wanted a hand out with a large parcel. Hume said, 'Don't put your hands underneath, hold it up by the rope,' but even then it was so heavy that it was slid down the stairs, and with some difficulty put into the car. According to the Prosecution, that was Setty's headless and legless body that was found on the Essex flats on 21 October. On the afternoon of 6 October, Hume drove to Southend with this parcel, and with some difficulty got it into the plane. He refused assistance, and put it on to the co-pilot's seat. When he arrived at Gravesend at 5.45 pm, there were no parcels.

Then there is silence for a while, Hume no doubt thinking that he had heard the last of it. On 12 October he was inquiring interestedly for his carpet, saying he wanted it for a party. On 14 October it was relaid in the flat, as it was later found by the police. But there is an old saying, and a true one, that murder will out. The largest parcel floated ashore, and on 21 October a farm labourer found it on the Essex marshes. He informed the police, and the police went and took the body to Chelmsford mortuary. It was there found to be wrapped up in underfelt secured by rope. The clothing was sufficient to identify it as the body of Setty. Dr Camps, the pathologist, found that death was due to shock and haemorrhage caused by five stab wounds in the chest.

MR HUMPHREYS *said that Setty was not wearing a waistcoat that day. The jacket was never found.*

Assuming that he was stabbed through his shirt and vest, which were on the body, it is of some importance that he had no waistcoat, and it is a matter of conjecture whether he was stabbed through the jacket. The weapon must have been at least one inch wide, double-edged, and four inches long. No such weapon was found in the flat. The body also had post-humous injuries which suggested that it had been dropped from an aeroplane. The head and legs were missing, having been sawn through. No saw was found at the flat. The doctor thought that the body had been put into the water some forty-eight hours after death, and had been about twenty-one days in the sea. That was a remarkable prophecy or opinion, because if Hume's story is right of when he disposed of the remains—and it will be seen that the murdered man was murdered on the night of the 4th—that was precisely forty-eight hours between the time of the murder and the body being put into the water—and if that is right, it was in the water from 6 to 21 October, which is not far short of three weeks.

On 26 October Hume was seen by the police, and when told that they were making inquiries about Stanley Setty he immediately replied: 'Oh, I can't help you with that. I know nothing about it.' That, of course, was a lie. He knew at least that he had taken part in the disposition of the remains. He told the police that he had driven for the last time three or four months previously; also a lie. He also said: 'I hired a plane that day to go to Southend, but I had no parcels with me; I only had my coat.' That was a lie. When the Inspector said: 'I have evidence to prove that you put parcels on the aircraft,' Hume, after saying, 'I am several kinds of a bastard,' gave a voluntary statement.

In the statement, Hume tells the story of dealings with a firm I will call Mansfield Autos, owned by a Mr Mansfield and a Mr Salvadori. Hume in his statement goes on to say that in the car mart he met three men, one described as 'Mac' or 'Max', somebody called Green or 'Greenie' or 'G', and another called 'The Boy'. He says that early in October these men approached him to fly things abroad and there was much telephoning and arguing about money. First the deal was on and then it was off, but on 5 October they said the plane was definitely wanted to fly things abroad. Between 2 and 3 pm on 5 October, Greenie and The Boy called with parcels to be deposited. Hume understood that the parcel contained plates of processed forged petrol coupons. They gave him bundles of £5 notes on account, and in the end some £150 in all. Those parcels, he said, were flown out and dumped. But on his return from the flight to his flat, the statement continues, Mac and The Boy were waiting with another parcel. This was the big one, which he put in the kitchen cupboard.

The statement then describes how on 6 October, Hume, with an employee from a firm called Saunders—that will be Staddon, the painter—carried the parcel to a car, and as he was carrying it down it made a gurgling noise. The statement goes on: 'I thought it was human body, that of a small man or a young person, and it crossed my mind that the package might have contained Setty's body, as I had read in the papers that he was missing.' Later, he compared numbers on the notes he had been given with those in a published list, and found that some of them corresponded with his own. The statement continues that he spent the evening of 4 October with a man named Muirhead in a public house in Shepherd's Market from six until nine.

That statement is very interesting indeed. It is true as to the disposal of the remains, where Hume knew that the police were in possession of the truth, but it is lies on a number of other particulars. It is a complete fantasy about three men, who do not exist outside Hume's fertile and romantic imagination. It is not true that those parcels were ever put into a kitchen cupboard; for if they were ever in the kitchen cupboard they left no stain, and therefore it is difficult to see how the parcels can have caused any other staining in the flat. It is not true that Hume needed a carving-knife, because Mrs Stride says there was no joint that day to carve. It is untrue that he spent three hours with a man named Muirhead on the night of the 4th, because Mr Muirhead says he never saw him that night at all, and he has never spent three hours, or anything like it, drinking with Hume. It is untrue that the three men called at his flat between 2 and 3 pm on 5 October, because Mrs Stride was there and she never heard the bell ring or anybody call. You may think that Hume is freely and cheerfully admitting that he is prepared to romance when it suits his purpose.

On the night of Friday, 28 October, Hume was charged with murder. The next day experts went to his flat and found it heavily stained with human blood, most of which was provably of the same blood group as that of the dead man. Blood was in the crevices of the floorboards. In the dining-room so much had been spilt that it had dripped through the boards to the plaster below.

Hume says the parcels were brought into the flat. The Prosecution will prove, so far as they can, they they were taken out of the flat, but there is no evidence that can be discovered that the parcels were taken in.

What happened on that night of 4 October I do not know, and it is no part of the case for the Prosecution to speculate. What does matter is this: Setty was murdered and cut up. I rely on no medical theory: I have no respect for any medical theory as to the details of matters which I do not have to prove and with which we are not primarily concerned, but it may be—I do not advance this as a theory upon which I can rely, and I care not if it be completely disproved—it may be that Setty was stabbed in the sitting-room near the door. He would immediately cough, and the blood would dribble out pretty fast from those wounds. That may account for the blood on the carpet near the door and the bloodstains still found on the floor near the door. Somehow he may have got across the hall, bleeding fast, to the dining-room; he may there have collapsed on his face on the floor where so much blood was found, and there died. Later the murderer, bloodstained, would have to go to the bathroom to wash himself and other things. There was blood in the hall, blood on the stairs and blood in the bathroom. The body would have to be cut up— the body of a 13-stone man—somewhere in the flat, and parcelled up. The parcelling up, you may think, was done— or a large part of it—in the kitchen on the afternoon of the 5th, when the defendant demanded the kitchen to himself for an hour and would not let Mrs Stride come in.

You may think one of the most difficult problems facing any murderer is the disposal of the body. But the defendant had almost unique opportunities because he could fly. So he flies, and drops those parcels, as he thinks, in the sea forever. He must have hoped against hope they would never return. But they did return, members of the jury, or part of them, on the returning tide. And that is why we are trying Brian Donald Hume for murder.

EVIDENCE FOR THE PROSECUTION

POLICE CONSTABLE THOMAS WALTER MACINDOE *provided a plan which he had prepared of the flat, 620B Finchley Road, Golders Green.*

CHIEF INSPECTOR PERCY LAW, *Photographic Department, New Scotland Yard, testified as to photographs he had taken of the flat.*

MRS EVA HABIBA OURI, *living at 53 Maitland Court, Lancaster Terrace, said that her brother, Stanley Setty, lived with her at her flat. She last saw him alive between 5 and 5.30 pm on 4 October, when she noticed his car and stopped to speak to him. She expected him back that night. Shown some clothes by Detective Inspector Davies, she recognised them as those worn by her brother on 4 October.*

STANLEY HINKS LAYTON, *cashier at the Yorkshire Penny Bank, Cheapside, said that on 4 October he cashed a cheque for £1,005 for a customer named Lewis, and Lewis handed the money in £5 notes to a man whom he now knew to be Isadore Rosenthal. The bulk of the money was in 200 new*

£5 notes of the series M41 consecutively numbered from 039801.

ISADORE ROSENTHAL, *a motor salesman, of 44 Genesta Road, Westcliff-on-Sea, said that as a result of seeing Setty on 5 October he went to the Yorkshire Penny Bank, Cheapside, with a Mr Lewis and cashed a cheque for £1,005. The money was in £5 notes, and he took it back to Warren Street, where he handed it to Setty.*

Cross-examined by MR LEVY:

Are you sure the date was 5 October?—Yes. It was a Tuesday.

MR JUSTICE LEWIS: Tuesday in that week was 4 October.

MR LEVY: Is Warren Street a place where deals are made in cars which have something possibly tainted about them?—Well, there are rumours, but we usually get to know which cars are tainted and which are not.

It is the recognised centre for illicit car deals?—Well . . .

WILLIAM JOHN MANSFIELD, *living at 1 Stockton Gardens, Tottenham, a director of Mansfield Autos of Fitzroy Street, gave evidence that he introduced Hume to Setty in October or November 1947.* MR HUMPHREYS *then read the descriptions of three men from Hume's alleged statement. In reply to counsel's questions as to whether he knew any persons answering those descriptions, the witness replied that he did not.*

Cross-examined by MR LEVY:

Suppose you were asked to help the police in identifying a gang of men who you knew would not stop short of murder if they found that you had given them away, would you be very anxious to help the police?—I think so, yes.

Were you warned to keep quiet about these things because the men that they were seeking might be violent?—I don't think I was. No, I was not. Not by the police.

Were you warned by anyone else?—No, I don't think so.

You know, don't you?—I was never warned about them.

ROY FRANCESCO SALVADORI, *living at 8 Beaulieu Gardens, Winchmore Hill, a co-director of Mansfield Autos, said that he knew Setty and Hume because of their transactions in cars. He did not know anyone named Mac or Max, or The Boy, but he knew a man named Green and had already told the police about him.*

MARTIN COLLINS, *greengrocer, living at 22 Sandringham*

Road, Golders Green, said that he was the owner of the shop on the ground floor of 620 Finchley Road, having taken over the business in January 1949. Five or six days after 1 October Hume paid the rent with a £5 note. Witness noticed that Hume had quite a lot of £5 notes. It was the first time Hume had paid with a £5 note.

Cross-examined by MR LEVY, *as to whether he had seen three men go to Hume's flat, Mr Collins said that he had not. Asked whether he had told anybody that he had seen men going up to the flat, the witness replied that he had seen one foreign-looking man.*

HENRY DOUGLAS MUIRHEAD, *living at 11 Upper Park Road, Hampstead, said that he did not meet Hume at a public house in Shepherd's Market at about 6 pm on 4 October. He had met him at other times.*

ERNEST FRANK SAMUDA BAILEY, *of 5 West Way, Pinner, an accountant at the Midland Bank, Golders Green, said that on 5 October Hume paid in a cheque for £90, and made arrangements to overdraw the account.*

MRS FRANCES LINDA HEARNDEN, *of 34 Prince's Park Avenue, Golders Green, manageress of Burtol Cleaners, 618 Finchley Road, said that Hume brought a carpet to her to be cleaned and dyed on 5 October; he did not want to unroll the carpet in the shop. He called several times and telephoned the factory twice before he got the carpet after fourteen days.*

MAURICE DAVID EDWARDS, *of 1 Russell Road, West Hendon, a panel-beater at Saunders Garage, Golders Green, identified a carving-knife which he said Hume gave him to sharpen on 5 October. Hume said to him: 'The joint is on the table and I want to get back quickly.' After cutting a rough edge on the knife, witness offered to complete it on an oil stone, but Hume said: 'No, it'll do.' Asked if Hume was always in a hurry to get things done, Edwards said that it was Hume's nature that he was here today and gone tomorrow.*

MRS ETHEL STRIDE, *of 44 Sheath Avenue, Golders Green, the Humes' cleaning woman, said that Mrs Hume had a baby on 17 July. Soon after her arrival at the flat after lunch on 5 October, Hume asked her to go out to buy a floorcloth, saying that he had used hers to wash a stained carpet. She noticed that the sitting-room carpet and a hall rug were missing.*

Hume said that the carpet had been sent away for cleaning, and that the surround of the sitting-room floor was going to be varnished. She did not see any men in the flat that afternoon, nor anyone bringing parcels to the flat.

MR HUMPHREYS: Did Hume go into the kitchen?—He said he was tidying up a cupboard in the kitchen to make room for coal to be stored for the winter, and he said he did not want to be disturbed.

On no account and in no circumstances?—They were his words, as near as I can remember. He did not wish to be disturbed, even to answer the telephone, and if it rang I was to say he was not at home. Mr Hume was in the kitchen about an hour and then he went out. He took two parcels with him, carrying one under each arm. They were roughly round parcels.

Asked to indicate the size, the witness held up her hands about 18 inches apart.

Did you see any signs of a joint in the flat that day?—No.

Cross-examined by MR LEVY:

I suppose you did not look for a joint?—No, it would be most noticeable in these days.

The witness said there were no signs of a body or anything that might be associated with death. She served Hume with a cup of tea at 3.50 pm, when she went into the kitchen.

Did you hear any noise like the sawing up of bones?—No.

In reply to MR JUSTICE LEWIS, *Mrs Stride said that Mrs Hume went out between 2.30 and 2.45 pm to take the baby for a walk, and had not returned when the witness left at 5.30.*

WILLIAM DAVEY, *of 188 Watling Street, Park Street, Hertfordshire, an aircraft fitter employed at Elstree by the United Services Flying Club, said that Hume arrived there on 5 October with two parcels and put them in an Auster aircraft. One was about 2ft 6in square, and the other about 18in square. He then took off.*

JAMES SMALL, *employed at Southend Airfield, said that he saw Hume land an Auster there at about 6.30 pm on 5 October. Hume told him that he had lost his way and had come down in bad weather. Later the witness taxied the machine to a hangar. There were no parcels in it.*

JOSEPH THOMAS STADDON, *of Crown Terrace, Cricklewood, a painter and decorator, said that on 6 October Hume asked him to stain part of the sitting-room floor. He did so, and stained part of another one. Hume asked the witness to help him carry a parcel downstairs and into his car. It was about 2ft 6in long, roughly 18in wide and 1ft high. It was very heavy, and the witness could not have lifted it himself.*

MR HUMPHREYS: Did you notice anything under the parcel, as of anything moist coming through?—No. I was going to put my hands underneath it and lift it down, but Hume stopped me and told me to carry it by the rope.

Did he say why?—He said it was valuable property. We lifted it a little way and when we had got nearly to the bottom I think Hume made a false step. I could not help it, but it slid down.

At the conclusion of STADDON's *evidence, the jury were taken to Hume's flat, which they examined for about fifteen minutes.*

SECOND DAY   *Thursday, 19 January*

It was announced that MR JUSTICE LEWIS *had been taken ill. The hearing was taken over by* MR JUSTICE SELLERS. *The jury was discharged and a new one sworn.* MR CHRISTMAS HUMPHREYS *said that the jury would try the case on evidence and not on speeches of counsel; therefore, in the special circumstances, he need only very briefly explain the case for the Prosecution. When* MR HUMPHREYS *had done so, witnesses who had given their evidence the previous days were recalled.*

The proceedings were interrupted when a telegram was handed to MR LEVY. *After consultation with* MR HUMPHREYS, MR LEVY *said that he thought it was a matter that the Judge would wish to deal with. The jury were then asked to retire.* MR LEVY *handed the telegram, and later a letter, to* MR JUSTICE SELLERS, *explaining that they had been sent to an important witness for the defence, Mrs Hume, by* MR DUNCAN WEBB, *a crime reporter on* The People, *care of the solicitors, who had obtained Mrs Hume's permission to open them.*

MR LEVY: It appears that a national newspaper is bringing pressure to bear on Mrs Hume not to give evidence. Your Lordship may think that this is a most unwarrantable and improper attempt to affect the course of justice.

MR HUMPREYS: I can only agree with my friend's complete and utter condemnation of such outrageous conduct. I offer to my friend protection to that witness day and night until she has given evidence.

MR DUNCAN WEBB, *summoned to the Court, agreed that he was the sender of the telegram and letter.*

MR JUSTICE SELLERS: Have you any explanation to give the Court?—My Lord, I have an explanation. Since this case has been on—that is, since Mr Hume has been arrested—I have been in constant touch with Mrs Hume, and the last time I saw her was as recently as last Friday.

How long have you known Mrs Hume?—I met her once about a year ago.

When did you next see her?—Two weeks after Hume was arrested.

In what circumstances?— What was your association with her?—Purely social.

Would it be right to say your association with her was as a newspaper man?—Not quite correct.

Tell me what is correct?—Mrs Hume told me several newspapers were asking her to write an article under her own name. I advised her not to do so.

Why did you act as you have? I have read the telegram and I have read that letter.—Yesterday I was talking to Mrs Hume's mother and she told me her daughter had been spirited away.

What had that got to do with you?—Mrs Hume had asked me to see her about the trial or at the end of the trial. I gather she is involved in this case.

What has that to do with you? What interest is it of yours? —I was asked by her mother and by her to be her escort.

What have you to say about this interference?—I was acting as her friend.

Do you know that in Common Law it is a misdemeanour to interfere with a witness?—I humbly apologise. I did not understand she was a witness in this trial.

*The witness said that Mrs Hume had been asked to write
an article of a certain nature, and her mother asked him if
he could use his influence to stop her writing it. He was in
no way attempting to interfere with her attendance at Court
or her giving evidence. Had he dreamed she was going to
give evidence, he would never have thought of writing to
her in that way. He had had too much experience to dream
of doing such a thing.*

MR JUSTICE SELLERS: On that explanation I will say nothing
more about this, but you should be reminded that to interfere
with a witness is a Common Law misdemeanour.

The case for the Prosecution then continued.

DR WALTER MONTGOMERY, *of the Metropolitan Police Laboratory, New Scotland Yard, said that on 27 October he
examined two cars—a black Singer saloon and a black Austin
12, which were shown to him by the police. He found no
evidence of bloodstains in them.*

SIDNEY TIFFIN, *of Tillingham, Essex, farm labourer, said
that he found a bundle floating in the water at Dengie Flats,
about 15 miles from Southend, on 21 October:* I went to it
and cut the cord, and inside I saw a body. I tied it to a stake
which I drove into the mud, and went straight to the police.

GODFREY MARSH, *of 17 Lincoln Road, East Finchley,
chauffeur at Saunders Ltd of Golders Green, said that at 9 am
on 6 October he drove from Golders Green to Elstree airfield
accompanied by Hume, who had two parcels. One was oblong
and looked like a carpet tied at the ends and in the middle
with string; the other was smaller and covered with brown
paper. Hume transferred the parcels to a Singer car at Elstree,
saying that he was in a hurry to get back to take his wife and
baby to hospital. Witness did not know what happened to
the parcels after they had been transferred to the Singer.*

Cross-examined by MR LEVY:

I suggest you are quite wrong about these parcels, and that
all Hume had with him was his overcoat?—He had two
parcels with him.

PETER ALAN YEOMAN, *of 21 Tudor Gardens, Leigh-on-Sea,
Chief Inspector at Southend Municipal Airport, said that on
6 October he saw Hume load a large parcel into an Auster
aircraft.*

JAMES JOSEPH RAYFIELD, *of 34 King's Drive, Gravesend, a metal-worker employed at Gravesend Airport, said that Hume landed there in an Auster on the evening of 6 October. He was carrying a green canvas bag and a raincoat, but no parcel.*

THIRD DAY

Friday, 20 January

DR HENRY SMITH HOLDEN, *director of the Metropolitan Police Laboratory, New Scotland Yard, said that on 25 October he examined an Auster aircraft at Elstree. He found traces of blood on the floor behind the left-hand seat. At Hume's flat he found stains caused by human blood on one corner of the green sitting-room carpet; the carpet had been cleaned and dyed. There were traces of blood in the hall over the whole surface of the linoleum, especially where the linoleum had been worn away. In the sitting-room he found blood in the crevices between the floorboards near the hall door. There were traces of blood in the bathroom. Below the dining-room floorboards he found blood on the lath-and-plaster ceiling of the room below; an appreciable quantity of blood had dripped through the crevices of the boards. He also found slight traces on several of the stairs leading to the bathroom, and on the bathroom linoleum. He could not say whether the blood on the stairs and in the bathroom was human blood or not.*

Cross-examined by MR LEVY, *the witness said that he had not detected blood on the pile of the sitting-room carpet, but only the under-part.*

How do you account for that?—I think it possible that the pile would clean more easily than the binding material underneath.

Do you know that the carpet was at all times laid upon underfelt? If blood was spilt on that carpet while it was laid on underfelt it would be inevitable, would it not, that some would get on the underfelt?—I should have expected it.

The witness said that he had found no trace of blood on the underfelt. Questioned about bloodstains in the coal cupboard in Hume's flat, the witness said that he examined it first on 31 October and there was quite an old spider's web there, from which he inferred that the cupboard had not been disturbed for a long time. Boards from the cupboard were handed to the witness. After examining them closely he said that he did not see any stains on two of the boards, but on a third board there was a red stain which could be blood.

Re-examined by MR HUMPHREYS, *the witness said that it would take time before blood seeped through to the base of the carpet, and from the base to the underfelt.*

WILLIAM JOHN MANSFIELD *(recalled) said, in answer to* MR LEVY, *that about a year ago a case was brought against himself, Mr Salvadori, Mansfield Autos Limited, and another motor company by the British Motor Traders Association for breaches of covenants on the purchase of cars. An injunction was granted against the defendants, restraining them from inducing other people to commit breaches of their covenants. Hume gave evidence for the Association against him.*

Did you resent that?—No, because Hume's evidence was that he offered a car for sale and was glad to get rid of it.

DR FRANCIS E. CAMPS, *pathologist, of 79 Harley Street, said that on 22 October he made a post-mortem examination on the trunk of a man's body. The cause of death was shock and haemorrhage due to multiple stab wounds. Death was caused rapidly, in a matter of minutes. The wounds were inflicted before death.*

MR HUMPHREYS: How many stab wounds were there in the chest?—There were five main stab wounds in the chest.

Will you just describe where they were?—One was situated just below the collar-bone, the direction being outwards and slightly downwards, into the soft tissues here (indicating) but not penetrating the chest cavity at all. Then there was a second wound, internal to that, cutting the rib and penetrating the upper lobe of the lung. There was a third wound below that, going through the second space between the ribs and penetrating the lung in a rather vital space, because it is recognised that the closer to the central part of the lung, the higher the mortality and the more rapidly death occurs.

Where was the fourth wound situated?—This was just inside the nipple, going laterally downwards and outwards —in fact, they all went downwards and outwards—again penetrating the lung. Finally, and lower still, there was a wound which went into the belly cavity between the muscle dividing it and the chest.

Were there cuts in a vest and shirt which covered the body, coincident with those cuts in the flesh?—Yes.

Witness thought the weapon must have been two-edged, about 1in in width and at least 4in in length. The trunk weighed about 110lb. Asked for his opinion as to how long after death it was that the body was put into the sea, the witness replied about forty-eight hours.

Cross-examining, MR LEVY *suggested that Setty was held when he was attacked, or at least that for some reason his hands were not free, otherwise there would have been defence wounds on them. He suggested that (a) Setty might have had his hands in his pockets or (b) he was being held by someone who was not the person who was stabbing him.* DR CAMPS *agreed that those were two possibilities, in the absence of a coat. He said that the only way in which a man could receive such stab wounds was if his coat was open.*

MR LEVY: You mean that they would not go through the coat?—They could, but I doubt it. They could go through with the coat half-open. Again, his hands could be fixed by his coat.

You mean that the coat could be drawn over his shoulders? —Yes, as a means of immobilisation.

MR LEVY *suggested that if Setty's hands had been free, he would have lashed out and struggled. The witness replied that Setty obviously did not lash out, because, had he done so, he would have received defence wounds.*

That is why I am suggesting to you that the mere fact that he did not lash out makes it very probable that the attack was by a number of persons and not by one person?—That may well be, but there is no evidence, from my findings, to support it.

But the evidence is consistent with that, is it not?—No.

Why not?—In the absence of any bruising of him being held.

Would that cause bruising, the arms being held?—Yes, it might well do so if they were held strongly or firmly.

We have often, I suppose, had our arms held without seeing any bruises?—Yes, at the time, but I think it is recog-

nised that we always look at bodies twenty-four hours afterwards, and bruises come up later.

Supposing his arms had been held behind?—Very firm
holding would show bruising.

MR JUSTICE SELLERS: With struggling as well?—Yes, I do
not say a gentle sort of thing.

MR LEVY: I suggest there would be a lot of struggling. If
there were only one assailant, a struggle would be almost
inevitable, with a great deal of noise?—I think it depends
upon what I said before. It is conjecture, because we do not
know what happened, do we? I think it is quite consistent
with a single assailant.

And you think it is equally consistent with there being a
number?—Yes, there might have been a number.

Re-examined by MR HUMPHREYS: Can you think of any
way in which the parcel of that man's trunk bound up in felt
could have made the stains that were found in the flat in
different places?—No.

DETECTIVE SUPERINTENDENT COLIN MACDOUGALL, *New Scotland Yard, said that a search had been made for three men
answering to the description of men referred to in a statement made by Hume. A man named Green was found.*

MR HUMPHREYS: Did he answer the description of any of
those three men?—Absolutely dissimilar.

Did you later find some other man, not of the name or
names given, but vaguely answering the description of one of
those men?—I did, sir.

Did you satisfy yourself that he had no connection whatsoever with this case?—I did, sir.

*The witness said that on 28 October Hume made a long
statement, which was taken down in writing and signed by
him.*

The statement, read by THE CLERK OF THE COURT, *said that
Hume during the World War II served for eighteen months
in the RAF and had a few hours' instruction in flying. At the
beginning of 1949 he joined the United Services Flying Club,
Elstree, to become an efficient pilot. Eventually he could fly
solo, but he had only one hour's instruction in map-reading
and, if flying in bad visibility, would have difficulty in finding
his bearings. The statement continued:*

(*left*) Brian Donald Hume with the dagger which, according to his 'confession', he used to stab Stanley Setty (*Syndication International*)

(*below*) Hume's sketch-map of his two flights over the Channel (*Syndication International*)

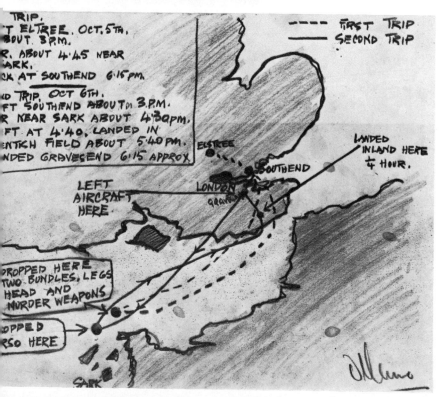

TRIP.
T ELTREE. OCT. 5TH.
OUT 3 P.M.
R. ABOUT 4.45 NEAR
ARK.
CK AT SOUTHEND 6.15 PM

D TRIP. OCT 6TH.
FT SOUTHEND ABOUT 3.P.M.
R NEAR SARK ABOUT 4.30PM,
FT AT 4.40, LANDED IN
ENTISH FIELD ABOUT 5.40 PM.
NDED GRAVESEND 6.15 APPROX

---- FIRST TRIP
SECOND TRIP

ELSTREE
SOUTHEND
LONDON
GRAVESEND

LANDED INLAND HERE ¼ HOUR.

LEFT AIRCRAFT HERE.

ROPPED HERE TWO BUNDLES, LEGS HEAD AND MURDER WEAPONS

OPPED SO HERE

SARK

(*left*) Trudi Sommer, who became Hume's fiancée during his period in Switzerland (*Syndication International*)

(*right*) Hume being led off by Swiss police after the Zurich bank robbery and the shooting of Arthur Maag (*Syndication International*)

About three years ago I bought a car, and after I had had it for about four months I sold it to Mr Mansfield and Mr Roy Salvadori. These men, I believe, sold the car to Saunders Garage in Golders Green. Salvadori paid me £1,250 for the car in £5 notes. There was trouble about me selling the car while it was under covenant.

I became friendly with Roy Salvadori, his brother Oswald, and Mr Mansfield. The British Motor Traders Association took civil action against several motor traders for buying cars sold under covenant. During these proceedings I got to know several of the dealers in Warren Street. Since then I have visited Warren Street several times and always called in Salvadori's office. I told both the Salvadoris and Mr Mansfield and several other motor traders that I could fly a plane. I did romance to them as to my capabilities as a pilot. While going to Salvadori's office I saw a man I know as Max or Mac. He is about 35, 5ft 10in or 11in, heavily built, clean-shaven, fresh complexion, fair hair parted in centre and brushed right back, who wears a large stone ring, I think on his right hand, and usually suede brogue shoes.

On Friday, 30 September, I was in Salvadori's office in the afternoon. Salvadori's office is in the basement, and on leaving the office and getting to the top of the stairs I met the man Mac, who was alone. He asked me if I was a flying smuggler and I said 'yes'. He led me into a room where the man Green was sitting. Mac said to him, 'This is him.' I also know him as 'G'. He is about 31 or 32, of dark complexion, with a black moustache. Should take him for a Cypriot. Mac said there would be some money for me if I could keep my mouth shut. He asked me if I could hire a plane that would carry five or six people without worrying about the customs.

They asked what type of plane it would be, and I told them it would be single-engined. Mac asked me if I knew a man named Salvadori, and I told Mac that I did. He told me he would be getting in touch with me.

On 2 October Mac telephoned me at home. My wife answered it. Mac said, 'You are not fucking us about over this plane?' and I said, 'If you want a plane you will have to find some money first.'

On 3 October Mac rang me in the evening and said he could do with a single-engined plane, and I told him I would have to have some money and he said he would fix all that.

On 5 October, at about 10 am, Mac said he wanted the

plane that morning. I was fairly well known at Elstree air-field, and went in a car I hired for twenty-four hours. Between 2 and 3 pm on 5 October Mac, Green and 'The Boy' called at my address. They had two parcels with them. I let them in. I do not know whether my wife was there. Mac said it would be better for me if I kept my mouth shut and I said I could do that all right.

He said he had some forged petrol coupon plates he had been making and wanted to get rid of them, and said they were hot. He inferred they were in the parcel they had brought to my home. I said it was an expensive way to get rid of them, and offered to hide or bury them. They discussed it and they said they wanted them dumped in the sea.

Green offered to go with me, but I said 'no'. He put one of his hands into one of his mac pockets and showed me a pistol or revolver. The Boy said he would fix this now, and pulled out a large roll of notes and said he would pay me. Green pulled out a bigger bundle and paid me ten £5 notes. I was impressed. I was to take the two parcels up in the plane and throw them into the English Channel. Mac said it would be unwise for me to interfere with them (meaning the parcels), and they left my flat.

Mac said, 'We will pay you another £50' as they went away. One of the parcels was about 15in square and wrapped up like a cardboard box and secured with rope. The other parcel was about 2ft 6in tall and 2ft thick, and round the outer cover was corrugated paper. It was securely tied with cord. It was heavy, and when I squeezed it it felt soft.

While the parcels were in my house after the men left them I put them in the cupboard in the kitchen of my flat. I would not know whether any stains had been left on the floor. I feel sure my wife did not see the parcels at any time while they were in the flat. I do not think my wife knew the men had been to the house. I did not tell her of the arrange-ments I had made regarding the disposal of the parcels. At 3.30 the same day I placed the parcels in the back seat of a car I had hired and drove the car to Elstree airport. At the air-port a groundsman carried one of the parcels and I carried the other and put them in the plane beside the pilot's seat. Before I left the airport I paid the cashier £20 in £5 notes in settlement of an outstanding amount.

I took off from Elstree at 4.30 and flew towards Southend. I continued out to sea and in a quarter of an hour turned

towards the Kent coast. Just before I turned I opened the
door and held the controls with my knees. I threw both
parcels out of the plane into the sea. I was at about a thousand
feet and four or five miles from Southend pier. I flew back
to Southend airport. I left the plane at the airport, and
returned by car to meet the men at Golders Green as
arranged. I paid the driver of the car with a £5 note. When
I got home Mac told me I was late and I told him I had
dumped the parcels in the sea. I did not tell him it was
between Southend and the Kent coast. Just before this I saw
the three men in a car outside my flat. I noticed in the back
seat was a bulky package.

I told Mac I had already spent about £30 and I had only
about £70 left for myself. Mac said, 'We are going to give you
a chance of earning another £50 tonight. We want you to
take another parcel and dump it in the sea tonight.' I told
them I could not, and I said I did not think it would fit into
the aeroplane. Mac said, 'You have started the job and you
will have to finish it', and The Boy said, 'You won't get any
more unless you do finish it.' I told them they would have
to take me to Elstree.

The Boy gave me £100 and told me to arrange to keep
the package upstairs until the next day. I agreed to take it to
Southend the following day. The Boy gave me £90 in £5
notes and £10 in £1 notes. It was carried into my flat. I told
them that one of them would have to help me carry it out
tomorrow to get it into the car, and they left the flat. By
this time I was afraid of the three men and because of this
I carried out their instructions.

The following morning, 6 October, I got to Elstree after
I had placed the bundle in the car. While I was taking it
downstairs it made a gurgling noise and I thought it was a
human body, and it crossed my mind it might have been
Setty's body, as I had read in the papers he was missing. I
knew Setty because I had sold him a Pontiac two years ago.
The parcel was 4ft tall, 2ft across, and 2ft thick. It was roped
up in Army blankets.

The bundle had give in it: the blankets must have been
sewn up as there were no loose ends. It took me all my time
to lift it. It was put into the back of the car and I drove to
Southend. I moved the package into the seat beside the pilot
and took some oil and went out to sea about the same
distance as on the previous occasion. I tried to drop the

parcel from the plane by putting the package against the door. I managed to get the door open. I took my hand from the controls and the plane went into a vertical dive and the parcel fell out into the sea. And then I lost my way and landed in a field in Kent. I took off and landed at Gravesend airport.

I returned home by car on the morning of 7 October. I had seen in the newspapers the numbers of a number of £5 notes connected with Setty's disappearance. I checked the numbers against the notes given me by The Boy. Four of them were identical.

On 23 October I read in the newspapers that Setty's body had been found at Essex. That night my telephone rang and The Boy asked me if I had read the Sunday newspapers. I have not seen any of the three men since 6 October.

SUPERINTENDENT MACDOUGALL *said that on 27 October Hume made a further statement, which read:*

I have been shown the wrappings found round the torso of Stanley Setty when it was found on the Essex coast. The material is similar to the wrapping of the large package which I put into the seat when I made the second trip with the plane. I cannot swear that it is the same because it is now wet, and was then dry.

SUPERINTENDENT MACDOUGALL *said that when Hume was searched, two pawn-tickets were found. One, dated 26 September, was for a suit, on which he had borrowed £1: the other, dated 1 October, was for a three-stone ring, on which he had borrowed £6.*

In cross-examination, MR LEVY *questioned the witness about the wording of Hume's statement:* What I am suggesting to you is that the words were very largely, if not entirely, your idea of the effect of the answers that he had given to your series of questions?—Not at all, sir.

Did he tell you he was afraid—he had been threatened and his wife and baby had been threatened?—Yes, he did, during the evening when I had taken a statement from him.

He was obviously worried, wasn't he?—Not at first he wasn't.

Did he not ask for police protection?—Yes, he did ask for police protection.

Would it be right to say that Setty was a well-known dealer in this black car market in Warren Street?—No. He was looked upon as quite an honest trader.

Has a careful and thorough examination been made for fingerprints and other marks at Hume's flat?—Yes.

Were any of the fingerprints found those of Setty?—No.

Were all Hume's clothes examined on the premises?—Yes.

Was there a single sign of a bloodstain on any of them?— No.

FOURTH DAY   *Monday, 23 January*

MR LEVY, *opening the case on behalf of the Defence, told the jury:*

The Prosecution say that some time, probably on the evening of 4 October, Stanley Setty was murdered, his body was cut up and was put into parcels, and those parcels were dropped from a plane into the sea. So far as those facts are concerned, you will probably have come to the conclusion that they are established to your satisfaction. They invite you to say that that murder and that cutting up were carried out by Hume. And they invite you to say that for a number of reasons. The two main reasons are that, first, they say, it is established that the three parcels containing parts of this man's body were dropped into the sea from an aeroplane by Hume. There again you may come to the conclusion that that fact is established to your satisfaction. They go on to say that bloodstains were found in Hume's flat. Therefore, they say, the presumption is that Hume, having disposed of this body, and there being bloodstains in his flat, murdered and cut up this unfortunate man. Members of the jury, you may feel that there is rather a long road between those facts and that conclusion.

According to the Prosecution, other circumstances point to my client's guilt. One of the circumstances, they say, is this: It is known that Setty had in his possession a large sum of money—something in the neighbourhood of £1,000 or more —and one of the most cogent motives for murder is robbery. That money undoubtedly disappeared after the murder of

Setty, and who is more likely to have murdered Setty for the purpose of robbery than Hume? Hume, they say too, was extremely hard up at that time—in grave financial difficulties. He had an overdraft, and, a few days before, had pawned articles for small sums of money. Of course he had an overdraft. He had had overdrafts before almost as big as this one, amounting to £50 or £60. Nobody has suggested before that he murdered anybody in order to reduce his overdraft. MR LEVY *said that on 3 October, the day before Setty disappeared, Hume paid his doctor £30 in £5 notes.* Do you think it was putting before you quite the complete picture of his financial position when that matter was not mentioned?

There are other circumstances on which the Prosecution rely. They say the names of the men—Mac, Green and The Boy— are mere fictions of the fertile imagination of Hume, and that these were people who did not exist. And what did the Prosecution put before you to satisfy you on that fact? They called two witnesses, Mr Mansfield and Mr Salvadori, and these two highly respectable gentlemen came into the witness-box to say 'We have never heard of anyone of these names. We don't know anyone of these descriptions!' Are these the sort of persons on whose evidence you could hang a cat, let alone a man? You will recall that judgment was entered against them in the High Court for conspiring to induce people to break their covenants with cars. Suppose those three men did exist and that Mansfield and Salvadori knew it well. If they knew that, they also knew from this story that those three men had murdered Setty. Do you think men of the calibre of Mansfield and Salvadori would risk their necks by giving information to the police about people they knew to be ruthless murderers?

I am in a position to put before you a very different state of things concerning the connections of that unfortunate man Setty. In the course of this trial, a great deal of evidence, including that of Mansfield, has been published abroad. It has come to the ears of someone who happens to know a great deal about the conditions in Cambridge Terrace Mews, where Setty had his garage. He has nothing to do with this case and he has never met Hume. He will give a picture of Cambridge Terrace Mews and this garage as a place where many cars go to be refurbished and repainted and re-cellulosed, and where many people go to visit Setty and his garage at all times. They were people of all kinds, some apparently quite normal and decent and reputable, but others apparently precisely the contrary, people who looked like thugs and 'spivs'. These were the sort of people who came to Setty's garage, apparently for business, and that is the background. I am not suggesting anything dishonest in Setty's dealings. I am referring to the background: the general business atmosphere that surrounded this unfortunate man: a background in which you may think rivalries and gangsterdom might well have had their birth. The case goes much further, because in that picture we find certain names occurring, names called out from one to another. Among those names was Mac or Maxie, and another was The Boy, and this witness who has come forward will tell you that stalking across this picture from time to time was a man whose description agreed closely with the description given by Hume of the man Green.

Hume does not pretend to be an angel; he *is* no angel. It may well be that Hume is the sort of man who goes about claiming to be more than he is. He may be an exhibitionist—but it is not every liar who is a murderer, assuming that Hume is a liar.

Another matter of which much was made is that Hume said that at one time this parcel containing the torso, which had been brought to him to dispose of, he had placed in the coal cupboard at the back of the kitchen. The Prosecution say that is another lie: that parcel—or any bloodstained parcel—was never in that cupboard, they say, because Dr Holden very carefully examined that cupboard and failed to find any bloodstains in it. Dr Holden went into the box—no more honest witness could be found—and I put to him that certain boards taken out of that cupboard were in fact stained with human blood. He admitted that they had every appearance of being bloodstained, and I shall prove that they were in fact stains of human blood. It thus appears that when Dr Holden said, 'I did not discover any blood in that cupboard,' what he meant was that he made a very cursory examination of one small part of the cupboard immediately behind the door.

I would ask you to keep in mind two times—5.50 pm on Tuesday, 4 October (when Setty was last seen), and between 3 and 4 the next day, because it was at that time that Hume took away from his flat two parcels and dumped them into the sea. I hope that you will see Mrs Hume in the witness box. She is a lady who had then recently had a baby. The baby at the time was about three months old, and Mrs Hume was living at home in the flat with her husband. She was breast-feeding the baby about every four hours. On the evening of Tuesday, the evening this man disappeared, some time between 6 and 7.30 pm on that evening (that is, almost immediately after Setty disappeared), Mrs Hume in the flat fed her baby. At 8 pm Mrs Hume was still in the flat. She would not know it but for one circumstance—that she remembers hearing a particular programme on the wireless. It was a very appropriate programme called *Justice in Other Lands,* and it dealt with the trial of a man known as the 'French Bluebeard', Landru.

On that very evening, if what the Prosecution tells you is right, Hume was in that flat murdering Setty. If he was murdered in this flat, he was murdered in the presence of Mrs Hume. She will tell you that certainly nothing happened in that flat during that evening that could remotely approach a murder or the cutting up of a body. Setty was a strong man. Do you think that a man like that could be stabbed to death five times from the front by a much smaller man, such as Hume is, without creating some commotion?

Dr Teare, the pathologist who is to be called for the Defence, will say that in his experience such a thing would be extremely improbable, and that if such a man was attacked in such a way he would almost certainly have defended himself, that there would have been a noise of scuffling, and furniture would have been turned over. If this man was seeking to stab to death another who was in his flat, do you think he would take the risk of going round and plunging the knife in at the front? If he was going to murder a man, it would have been his back in which he inserted the knife. Is there not only one conclusion that one can draw from this —that, as this man Setty was being stabbed in the chest, he was being held from behind? One man could never have committed this murder, and I suggested this to Dr Camps. He said: 'Oh no, if he had been held from behind there would have been bruises.' Do you think that it is impossible for a man to be restrained without bruising his arms?

There is another flat in the house, a flat underneath, occupied by a headmaster, Mr Spencer, and his wife. Their sitting-room is underneath Hume's flat. Mr Spencer was in all that evening, and there was no sound of any struggle going on. The next morning Mrs Hume was in the flat, with the possible exception of a short time when she was out shopping. Hume went to the bank some time between 10 and 11 am. Some time about mid-day something else happened. Unfortunately Mrs Hume's baby had been ill. The doctor called, either because he had been asked to call or because he was passing on this morning, 5 October. He went up to the nursery and he went into the bathroom to wash his hands and found no suspicious signs. He went into the sitting-room and chatted with Mr and Mrs Hume, and in the sitting-room he wrote a letter which he gave to Mrs Hume for the admission of her child to the Children's Hospital—where, in fact, the child was taken the next day. He did more than that. Mr Hume complained to him of sleeplessness, and Dr Blatchley gave him a prescription. Dr Blatchley will tell you that there were no abnormal signs about the flat at all.

Shortly after that, Hume went to the chemist to have the prescription made up, and remained there for twenty minutes. At about 12.30 pm he went to Burtol's about the carpet. Between then and 1 pm he took the carpet and left it to be dyed. Round about one o'clock, he took the knife to Saunders to be sharpened, and thereafter had his lunch and was there with his wife until Mrs Stride, the daily maid, came at two. MR LEVY *asked the jury to keep those times in their minds because they were times which were established by completely independent and disinterested evidence.*

What time during that morning do you think Hume could have had to cut up the body of Setty, and where could he have done it? At two o'clock Mrs Stride went through to the kitchen and there were no signs of disorder; she remained in the flat for some time. Supposing one accepts that it would take this man an hour to cut up the body; parcelling and tying up might take half an hour, and then you add the cleaning up of the filthy mess, and how long will that take? I submit that it was utterly impossible that the body could have been cut up in that flat.

Referring to the carpet which Dr Holden had said had a stain caused by human blood, MR LEVY *said:* The only scientific indication you have is that it may be human blood or it may be some other human secretion. Dr Holden has said in cross-examination that other human secretions could also have given a positive reaction, and Dr Holden thought that because it was so large it was more likely to be human blood. Apparently it is suggested that Setty was stabbed in the sitting-room. Suppose he were, and suppose his blood flowed down on to this carpet. There was so much, if it was blood, that it so impregnated the underbinding part of the carpet that even after cleaning and dyeing its presence could be seen and detected scientifically. All the time the carpet was resting on the underfelt, yet no blood has been found on the under-felt. What that stain is, goodness only knows. It is a stain of some human secretion, and that is as far as science can take it.

BRIAN DONALD HUME, *examined by* MR LEVY, *said that he was just under thirty years of age, married, and lived with his wife Cynthia and five-month-old daughter. During the war he served in the RAF and was given instruction in flying. About a year ago he joined the United Services Club at Elstree and got a pilot 'A' certificate. From time to time he had had dealings in motor-cars, which had brought him into touch with Mr Salvadori, and also with Mr Mansfield. He was known in the car market of Warren Street as the 'flying smuggler'. He was called for the plaintiffs in the High Court case against Mansfield and Salvadori; during the action he met a man whom he knew as Mac or Max.*

MR LEVY: Was he called by any other name?—I never found out correctly whether it was Mac or Max.

HUME *repeated the description of Mac, and then told of his meeting with Green, whom he described as:* about thirty-one or 32. His hair was brushed back and cut in a thick wave at the back, which somebody told me was a Boston haircut. He had a flashy green suit with exceptionally wide trousers, and

plain suede shoes. I should say his height was about 5ft 6in
or 5ft 7in. He wore a tight overcoat with a belt, and no hat.
I should say he was either a Greek or a Cypriot, and as he
mentioned early on that he had flown to Cyprus I took him
for a Cypriot. *Replying to* MR JUSTICE SELLERS, *he said that
the man he met later called The Boy called Green only by
the letter 'G'. He thought Mac was either a Scotsman or from
the Midlands. The first meeting lasted about half an hour.
He was next rung up on Monday, 3 October, by Mac, who
told him that he wanted an aeroplane. He told Mac that he
would want the money first, before he chartered one, and
was informed that that position was taken care of.*

MR LEVY: Did you mention how much it would cost? Had
anything been said up to this time about you being paid for
your services?—Oh yes, I was told that the deal was on and
that I would be included in it.

HUME *said that the man told him he would ring back in
about ten minutes, and when he did so he said he did not
want the aeroplane. He next heard from the man the next
day.* I understood originally that they wanted to go out of the
country, and I as good as suggested that it could be arranged.
The following day, Tuesday, 4 October, Mac rang and said
they definitely wanted the plane. He asked me if I had a car.
The way he put it at first I thought he wanted to buy that
particular type of car. Now he spoke about driving the car.
I said I did not have one, but I could get hold of one. I rang
the aerodrome and told them I thought I would want an
aeroplane. I did not propose to enter into any contract until
I had seen the colour of their money. They eventually came
round between two and three o'clock on Wednesday, 5
October. *On the morning of that day he paid £90 into his
bank.*

MR LEVY: Up to that time had you received any money
from Green or Mac or The Boy?—None at all, sir.

Had that £90 anything to do with this transaction?—No.

HUME *said that at that time his daughter was ill and Dr
Blatchley called. He spoke to him about his sleeplessness. The
doctor gave him a prescription and at about 12.15 he took it
to the chemist to be made up. He also went down and asked
the lady in the cleaners if she dyed carpets. After she had*

*shown him a sample of the colour he went upstairs, took up
the carpet and carried it down to her.*

MR LEVY: Why were you having the carpet dyed?—It was
always arranged that the carpet would be dyed. The carpet
was filthy.

If it be that on the back of the carpet there is a bloodstain,
do you know anything about it?—Nothing at all whatsoever.

Questioned about the carving-knife, Hume said: I had been
helping to get the lunch ready, laying the table or something
like that. I either had the carving-knife for the joint—I think
the butchers had been on strike and we were getting a back
allowance of meat—or I had an Alsatian which consumes
large quantities of horsemeat, which needs a fairly sharp
knife to cut. I cannot remember whether we did have a joint
or not that day. But it was one thing or the other. It was at
my wife's suggestion that I went to have it sharpened. She
was always getting on to me about it.

It is said you could not wait to have a proper edge put on
the knife because you were in a hurry?—The reason is that
we did have a joint that day and my wife had sent me down
to get it done quickly. I sort of rushed down there.

When Mrs Stride was in the flat did you say anything about
wanting to be in the kitchen?—After she had been in the flat
about half an hour, I told her that I was going to clear out
some things from the kitchen cupboard. The reason for
clearing it was to bring coal upstairs. The coalman would not
take the coal up to the kitchen unless someone was there and
tipped him.

Were you doing anything in the kitchen besides clearing
out the cupboard?—Not necessarily, but I had a deed-box,
and I had insurance policies due, and I think I sorted them
out.

Were you in the kitchen altogether doing these things for
about an hour?—About fifty minutes. *During that time Mac
and Green and another man he had not seen previously called
The Boy, called. The Boy was about 5ft 9in or 10in tall,
with brown hair, a receding forehead, sometimes wearing
steel-rimmed glasses and a very bright-coloured pair of brown
buckled shoes. He was about thirty-five. During the con-*

*versation he took out the glasses and put them on. They
brought two parcels. One was a square cardboard box. The
other was 2ft 6in long and wrapped in brown paper.*

I was told that these parcels contained forged petrol coupon
units or something very similar, and they told me to dump
them in the Channel. The petrol units were the iron presses
used to make the coupons. The police were after them. It was
agreed that the job was worth £100. I wanted paying the
whole lot in advance, but I was given only £50 in advance—
in £5 notes. A revolver was produced, and I was told that I
was not dealing with crooks from Hyde Park, or words of that
description. They said they would meet me that night about
a quarter to nine about the other £50. I put the parcels in
the kitchen.

MR JUSTICE SELLERS: Could you tell me what time you
think the men arrived?—I should say about 2.50; it may have
been 2.45. I think after my wife had gone upstairs to start
feeding the baby.

MR LEVY: Can you tell with any certainty whether it was
after the arrival of Mrs Stride?—(*The witness considered for
nearly a minute.*) No, I cannot remember.

HUME *then said that he went out of the flat with the two
parcels. He drove to Elstree airfield and the plane was ready.
He thought he put one parcel in the front and one on the
back, but could not be sure.* I took off and I flew on a course
towards the Thames, which is parallel to the runways of the
airfield. I flew at about 2,000ft and eventually I followed the
Thames until the end of Southend Pier. I did my take-off
about 5 or 5.15. By the time I turned back to the coast I
suppose it was about six o'clock, and I had a bit of a job to
see the ground, so I went in and landed at Southend airport.
I knew I should not get back to Elstree that night. I made an
arrangement to leave the plane there and I asked somebody
to taxi the plane into a hangar, to leave it there for a night.
Then I went to make arrangements about a hire car to take
me to London. They told me the driver was at his meal. I
went in to him and asked him to take me back so as to be in
time to meet these men.

The men drove me back to London, and I got to Golders
Green. Mac came up to me and I saw The Boy and Green in

a car. Also in the car was the third parcel. I told them I had dumped the parcels into the sea—in the Channel, I did not say the Thames Estuary—and I also told them it had already cost me about £30. I asked for my other £50 that was due to me. Before they gave it to me they told me they were going to give me a chance to earn another £50 that night. I was told that they wanted me to take this big parcel and drop it that night. But I told them I had not done any night-flying. I asked them first of all if they would drive me over to Elstree to put it in the back of my car. I explained that I had left the plane at Southend. It was eventually arranged that I would keep the parcel in the flat that night and drop it in the following day. *He was paid £90 in £5 notes and £10 in £1 notes. The car was driven round to the flat and Mac and The Boy carried the parcel up. As they were taking the parcel up the stairs he asked the men what it contained and they replied, 'The same as before', or something like that. The men put the parcel in the cupboard in the kitchen.*

MR LEVY: Did you do anything to the parcel after the men left?—I went to the cupboard to move it to the side. When I lifted it up it made a gurgling noise, and when I had moved it I saw a pool of blood underneath. I was frightened. Then I noticed blood in the dining-room where the parcel had rested. I wiped it up with the first cloth that came into my hands. I slept that night in the flat.

Hume said that it was usual for him to stain the floors of the flat two or three times a year. The next morning he brought the coal up. I turned the parcel on its back, which was the side the blood wasn't, and left it by the refrigerator. *His wife left to take the child to the hospital at 10, and he dragged the parcel at far as the scullery.* I picked it up and started walking through with it. In doing so I dropped it on the floor of the dining-room. One end of it opened up, and it squirted blood. I grabbed it and dragged it into the hall.

Did you do anything about the blood?—I did not do anything immediately. I readjusted the ropes at the edge of the parcel and went into the kitchen and got a large piece of brown material, and tucked it round it.

MR JUSTICE SELLERS: You got what piece of material from

the kitchen?—It was part of one of my wife's old frocks torn up, and I tucked it round.

MR LEVY: Did you do anything about the stains in the hall? —Yes, I wiped them up very quickly, and then Staddon, the painter, was coming up and I threw the rag into the dining-room and closed the dining-room door.

Hume then described how Staddon helped him down with the parcel.

MR LEVY: Is it right that you told him not to hold it underneath, but to hold it by the rope?—Yes, because I thought he might get blood or varnish on his hands. I took the parcel to Southend in the car, put it into the plane, took off and flew over Southend Pier. I dropped the parcel into the estuary.

When did you next see any of the three men?—I think it was the Sunday morning that Setty's body was found. It was the man Mac, I think, that rang me up and asked me if I was getting squeamish, as £1,000 had been offered as a reward. There were a number of things said. I said I supposed I was in it as deep as them, for 150 quid too. I was told to remember I had a wife and baby. *Since that conversation he had not heard from or seen any of the men. He said that the long statement to the police started at about 11 am and went on until about 11 pm. At first he denied dropping the parcels into the sea* 'because I thought there was something dodgy about it'.

MR LEVY: And later you asked for police protection?—I asked before I gave my story, and they gave it most definitely to my wife.

Why did you ask?—I had been threatened and I thought if I was going to spill the beans generally I had better get it laid on.

Have you ever had in your possession a knife one inch wide and four inches long, which it has been suggested was used for stabbing Setty?—No.

Did you murder Stanley Setty?—No, most definitely not.

Cross-examined by MR HUMPHREYS:

I want the jury to understand the man they are trying. On your own confession you were prepared to assist men who told you in terms that they were forgers of petrol coupons?—They did mention that, yes, sir.

And you believed it?—Yes, sir.

You were prepared, for money, to remove the traces of that crime?—Yes, sir.

By the time the second parcel arrived you believed they were murderers?—No, I did not, sir.

But when you took that second parcel out of the house it was squirting blood, you say?—I flew the body in a plane. They brought it to the house, but they are not necessarily the men who killed him.

What did you think it was?—I thought it might have been part of a human body.

It was obviously part of a human body, wasn't it?—No, sir, not obviously.

When Setty was missing?—I did not connect the two of them.

Didn't you? I suggest to you that you knew perfectly well. MR HUMPHREYS *then quoted from Hume's alleged statement.* 'It crossed my mind that the package may have contained Setty's body as I had read in the papers that morning that Setty was missing.'—I was asked if I had read it in the paper that morning, and I said yes, and that is what was put in the statement.

MR HUMPHREYS *also quoted*: 'While I was taking it downstairs it made a gurgling noise. I thought it was a human body of a small or young person. It crossed my mind that the package may have contained Setty's body, as I had read in the papers that morning that he was missing'—I had not read that statement before I signed it.

Why did you sign it?—Because it was half-past ten at night and I had had enough of the police that day.

You say that you did not connect the parcels with a human body?—No, sir.

What else could they have been connected with that spurts human blood unless it is a human body?—*The witness did not reply.*

What do you say now you believed you were disposing of in that parcel that was squirting blood?—When I first saw blood my attitude was—whatever it is, out! I was not prepared when first given the parcel to throw it into the sea. I was going to dump it somewhere. Then I thought how easy it

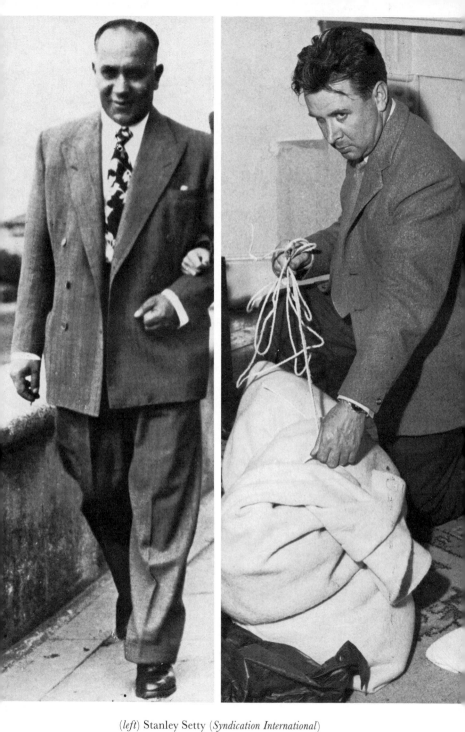

(*left*) Stanley Setty (*Syndication International*)

(*right*) Hume demonstrating how he tied up part of Setty's body (*Syndication International*)

(*above left*) Detective Superintendent Colin MacDougall (as he was then) in charge of the investigations into Setty's murder (*Syndication International*)

(*above right*) Mr Christmas Humphreys, QC, who led for the Prosecution at Hume's trial at the Old Bailey (*Barratts Photo Press*)

(*right*) Number 620 Finchley Road as it is today, almost unchanged externally from the time of the murder. The shop below is still a greengrocer's (*Francis Beuttler*)

was to get rid of the other two and I'll dump it into the sea from a plane.

You knew the parcels felt like parts of a human body?—Yes.

And you connected it with Setty?—I did not.

You had read that Setty had disappeared?—I had known Setty about two years.

You are still saying it never crossed your mind you were throwing Setty into the sea?—Definitely no.

How do you think the three men had been connected with a human body unless they were the murderers of it?—I did not realise it was a human body until after they had gone.

What did you think the three men were who had brought you a human body?—They could have been murderers.

What did you think about?—I did not look into the parcel.

Who was it first used the phrase 'flying smuggler'?—Mac.

Were you known as the 'flying smuggler'?—Evidently. It was just an expression. I had been connected financially in one or two aircraft that had gone out to the Middle East at the time the Arabs and Jews were fighting.

To smuggle?—No.

Would it be right to describe you as a romantic liar?—No, completely the opposite.

As a person prepared to lie when it suits you?—It would be completely wrong.

You were more frightened of the three men than of the security of the police?—If I had gone to the police and told them, they would not have believed me any more than they believe me now.

How do you know?—I know the police.

You have always set yourself up to be a great figure in the RAF?—No.

Do you know a woman called Theresa? I do not want to give her full name.—No, you can give it.

I don't want to give her full name, but she is a dancing teacher and called Theresa?—No.

Whom you have dined in a club in Knightsbridge?—No.

You have never described yourself as a Pan-American pilot?—I have not.

E

You are a member of the Wellington Club at Knights-bridge. You have taken this girl and dined there?—No.

Is her name Theresa?—I don't know anyone of that name.

But you are a member of the club and are known as 'the Captain'?—No.

And have given your address as Haigh Castle?—I don't know.

You have cashed a cheque and it has been returned RD?—I have never cashed cheques at the place.

Was one returned RD?—Yes.

Did your wife think you were earning a living as a pilot?—I was earning my living indirectly. I was connected with flying aircraft over to the Middle East.

How were you making your living at this time?—I was connected with aircraft that went to the Middle East.

What were you to get for it, and how much a week?—There was no money. They would perhaps get altogether something like £500 to £600 if an aircraft was sold. I was not hard up. I think I earned on these deals between £12 and £14 a week.

Who was the seller?—A man named Reginald Simpson, a representative of the Iraqi Government. We sold two planes about last May or June.

What did you get for that?—We sold two Ansons and altogether got £2,200.

Who are 'we'?—Another man and myself.

Who got the profit?—We split it. I say I made about £600.

MR JUSTICE SELLERS: Were you the owner of the planes you sold?—I was acting as an agent. The planes were surplus RAF machines and I was just a go-between.

MR HUMPREYS *asked Hume if in the RAF he had failed in his examinations and had not qualified either as a pilot or an air-gunner.* HUME *said he had been discharged through spinal meningitis from concussion he got in a crash.*

Did you, shortly after leaving the RAF, get into trouble with the police for wearing the uniform of an RAF officer?—Yes, I have admitted that.

I think you agree that your wife never saw these three men and that Mrs Stride never saw them?—I admit that.

You know the police have not been able to find these men?

You would have thought it would have been easy to spot them by the clothes which you have described them as wearing?—Not necessarily. They had a photo of the 'Mad Parson'* and did not find him, although he was living opposite Albany Street Police Station.

Referring to the first interview, MR HUMPHREYS *asked whether he thought the men were planning a murder*. HUME *replied:* 'No, sir. They gave me the impression that they were trying to get out of the country.'

The men who approached you were practically complete strangers. You never got to know anything more about them than that they are called Mac, Green and The Boy; and you ask the jury to believe they came to you and asked you to help them to dispose of a human body?—I repeat I know nothing about a human body.

If they had come to you like that, they would have been at your mercy, would they not? You could have phoned the police and they would have had the place surrounded?—No, I was scared stiff.

Why not, if you are an honest man?—I am not saying I am one hundred per cent honest. I am saying I am a semi-honest man—but I'm not a murderer. My attitude when I saw the large parcel was, 'This is something dodgy—so, out.' I had got rid of the first two parcels and I could get rid of the other in the same way.

FIFTH DAY
Tuesday, 24 January

BRIAN DONALD HUME *(recalled); cross-examination continued by* MR HUMPHREYS:

What cleaning of blood did you do, and of what stains?— I cleaned up the stains inside the coal cupboard and I also washed up some stains in the dining-room.

The big parcel which caused the stains on the boards in

*In 1947 John Edward Allen escaped from Broadmoor (to which he had been committed after strangling a seventeen-month-old baby girl), wearing a clerical collar which he had used as a prop in a concert party run by the inmates and called the Broadhumoorists. He remained at liberty for nearly two years, and became popularly known as the Mad Parson.

the dining-room was put down there. How was it taken to the cupboard? Was it lifted or dragged?—It was lifted, not dragged, by two of the men to the coal cupboard. At night I moved it.

Dealing with the coal cupboard, did you have any coal up between 5–6 October and 29 October?—Coal was brought up on 5 October by me.

And put over the stains in the coal cupboard?—Definitely not. The coal was put in the back where there was an empty space.

To the left inside the cupboard was where the bloodstains were found?—No, it was quite a big area in the cupboard.

Now, about the gurgling noise. Are you saying you did not say it gurgled when it went downstairs?—Yes, I am.

When you were near the bottom of the stairs, was the painter unable to hold the parcel any longer, and did he let it fall?—He let go of it and I went forward quickly with it and let it drop on the stairs themselves. I 'brushed in' the blood with fresh varnish.

How did the blood get in the hall?—I don't know.

How did the blood get inside the sitting-room?—I cannot explain it.

MR HUMPHREYS *referred to the carpet in the dining-room, and* HUME *said that the stain might have been caused by a child who had been staying in the house.*

MR HUMPHREYS: You were unwilling to open up the carpet when it was taken to the cleaners?—I was quite willing to open it. The woman had to price it according to the size of the carpet.

MR LEVY: The woman never said that he was unwilling to unroll the carpet. It is a complete misrepresentation, and my friend has no right to put distorted accounts.

MR HUMPHREYS (*to* HUME): You do not suggest that the stains on the corner of the carpet came from the blood on the parcel?—No.

I suggest that you stabbed Setty in the sitting-room and that he died in the dining-room?—Now you are romancing.

And that you cut him up that night?—Absolute baloney.

Have you any evidence other than your wife's that you were in the flat that night?—I have only my wife's evidence that I was in the flat. The same as on hundreds of other nights.

Plenty of time in which to cut up a body. You had a knife, is that right?—I had a carving knife.

MR HUMPHREYS *asked about 3 October, on which date Hume said he paid Dr Blatchley £30:* I suggest you borrowed that money from Setty?—Absolute baloney.

Early in October you were hard up, were you?—I was not hard up.

Cheques being returned RD by the bank?—One or two, yes, but they had been before.

Owing your hairdresser £9?—I certainly did not. That's a complete fantasy.

When HUME *started answering questions almost before* MR HUMPHREYS *had finished asking them* MR JUSTICE SELLERS *restrained him:* Just listen to the questions. Learned counsel is doing his duty in cross-examining you.

MR HUMPHREYS: Are you saying that you never borrowed money from the hairdresser?—I am saying that I did borrow money but that I paid it back to him, and now he owes me money.

What in the evidence that Mr Mansfield gave, as far as you can remember, can you dispute?—I dispute that he doesn't know the man called Mac.

Are you saying that he does?—Yes. He came back with us in a shooting brake after the case at the High Court.

MR JUSTICE SELLERS: Who were in the shooting brake with you?—The man Mac and Mansfield and Salvadori.

Questioned by MR HUMPHREYS *about the RD cheques at the club and arrears in rent while he had £280,* HUME *retorted:* You have got time and dates mixed up.

I am dealing with 3 October. Where did the money come from?—I had the money. I got some money from my father-in-law previously. £75 in £5 notes.

Where did you keep it?—I kept it in my pocket. I walked about with £280.

You pawned your suit for £6 when you had £280 in your pocket?—I don't know the dates of the tickets.

Why did you give an RD cheque at your club if you had money in your pocket?—I cannot explain that.

You have said that you were very urgent to have the knife sharpened?—Very likely the joint was on the table. My wife was in a hurry to get the dinner and feed the baby, and that is why I was in a hurry to get the knife.

Although you were in a hurry, you went down to the garage to have a knife sharpened to cut a joint which Mrs Stride could not find?—It could have been the remnant of a joint we had the previous day.

Did your wife wash up?—No. I think she went straight up to feed the baby.

Did you wash up?—No.

Mrs Stride said that when she arrived, the washing-up had been done?— (*No reply.*)

There was no time, was there, for these men to come and to do all that arguing and arranging before two o'clock?—I don't know about the time, but these men definitely did come on that day.

I suggest that you saw the red light from Mrs Stride's evidence and you changed the time to before two o'clock?— I am the one who knows whether I killed Setty or not, other than the men who murdered him. I have a clear conscience regarding the killing of the unfortunate man.

MR JUSTICE SELLERS: You are adopting this as a personal matter.—My life is a personal matter.

MR HUMPHREYS: There was no time for these three men to come before two o'clock without your wife knowing, was there?—My wife goes up usually at 1.30 pm, but she might have gone up at 1.20 pm for all I know.

When the men came, did they ring the bell which rings in the hall?—Yes.

Perhaps the jury have heard it. It makes a frightful noise right through the flat. You could not have failed to hear it?— You could. Mrs Stride may have been working upstairs with the vacuum cleaner.

Mrs Stride said no men came to that flat while she was there?—Mrs Stride can be mistaken. The men could have called before Mrs Stride arrived.

It is one of those two things?—Yes.

You tell Mrs Stride for the first time in your life she is not to interrupt you?—Not necessarily. I told her about answering the telephone bell.

She had said clearly you were not to be interrupted, not

even for the telephone. It was as urgent as that. What were you doing in the cupboard that Mrs Stride was not allowed to see?—She could have come into the kitchen if she wanted to. There was no lock or bolt on it. I was definitely clearing the coal cupboard out.

MR JUSTICE SELLERS: If these men came before two o'clock, they brought the two parcels with them?—Yes.

HUME *went on to say he put the parcels in the coal cupboard in the kitchen first of all, then under the kitchen table when he started to clear out the coal cupboard. His wife could have gone into the kitchen and seen them, but he did not think Mrs Stride would have entered the kitchen.*

MR JUSTICE SELLERS: On your own story, these parcels remained in the kitchen until you took them out under your arm at 4.10 pm?—Yes.

You will appreciate why all these questions are being put to you by counsel. It is being suggested that this did not happen at all, and that these men never came to your flat at all?—Yes, my Lord.

Do you suggest that they did, and that the parcels remained there in your flat for over an hour without your wife knowing anything about them?—Yes, definitely. My wife never went to the coal cupboard. There were mice in there and she was frightened of them.

Did you want to exclude Mrs Stride from the kitchen?—Only when I was working on the coal cupboard.

Did you ask her not to disturb you?—I think I said I was working in the coal cupboard.

Are you asking the jury to take the view that although there were two parcels in the kitchen, you were asking Mrs Stride not to disturb you because you were cleaning out the coal cupboard?—I was wearing short white trunks. I had taken my other clothes off. They were running or football trunks. I did not want to be seen walking round the flat in them.

And it had nothing to do with any packages?—No.

MR HUMPHREYS: Were you cutting up portions of Setty's body and parcelling it?—Definitely not.

MR HUMPHREYS: No further questions.

MR JUSTICE SELLERS: Do you ask the jury to accept you were not hard up, as suggested by the Prosecution, on 3 and

4 October?—I was not hard up to that extent. I had had an overdraft at the bank a number of times before. I had £280 on me on 3 October and had paid a doctor's bill for £30. There were going to be transactions with two aircraft. I had the £280 and I was trying to increase it to £300.

That is why you pawned your suit?—No, just a ring. I was not short of money.

Did you know the names of the three men or their addresses or anything about them?—No. I only knew the man Mac.

Did you know where to find him?—It was either taking the £50 or nothing at all.

Will you answer my question? Did you know where to find him?—No.

And you went off to do this task to get rid of what you ask the jury to believe you thought was forging apparatus? You had been paid £50?—I was originally only going to get £50 for the job. I asked for £100 and I thought they would beat me down to £50. I was prepared to get £50 in advance. I would have made about £45 profit.

You could never have found those men again?—No.

Did you tell your wife about the packages or the men coming to the flat?—No.

MRS CYNTHIA HUME *said that she married Hume in September 1948, and they had lived in the flat in Finchley Road ever since. Asked by* MR LEVY *about the carpet, she said they ordered a green one, but the firm did not have the shade they wanted, and they took what they had. The carpet in the sitting-room had become soiled and her husband had cleaned it. He had also stained the boards a number of times. The underfelt was the only one in the flat; she had not seen any other large pieces of felt in the flat. She fed her baby daughter five times a day, at 10 am, 2 pm, 6 pm, 10 pm and 6 am. She took the baby out each afternoon between 2 pm and 3.30 pm, and stayed out until about 5.45 pm. Dr Blatchley, who had care of the child, saw the baby on Monday, 3 October and on Wednesday, 5 October. On the evening of 4 October she heard a play.*

MR LEVY: Is there any particular play which you remember having heard about this time on the wireless?—I did not remember it until I was given to understand that I might remember from the *Radio Times*. I do remember that the play was about the French 'Bluebeard'. I remembered the programme through a photograph of Landru, the subject of the play.

MR LEVY *handed a copy of the* Radio Times *to the witness, who identified the photograph.*

MR LEVY: I think the play was called *Justice in Other Lands* and that this broadcast was about Landru. I shall prove by other means that this play purports to have been broadcast on 4 October between eight and nine in the evening. (*To the witness*): Do you remember whether your husband was at home or not on that particular evening?—No.

Have you ever met Setty?—No.

So far as this particular night, Tuesday, 4 October, is concerned, can you recollect one way or the other whether he actually came to bed with you or not?—I don't know. I imagine he did, but I cannot say for certain.

If he did not come to bed, say, for hours, do you think you would have known it, or remembered it?—I think I would be more likely to remember it.

Would it have been possible, do you think, for your husband to bring anyone to that flat in that period, sometime between six and eleven on that night, and murder him in the flat—and murder him without you knowing anything about it?—Quite impossible.

Did you hear any sound or any commotion or anything that could posibly suggest any such happening while you were in the flat?—No.

MR LEVY *referred to the following day, Wednesday, 5 October.* MRS HUME *said that on the morning of that day the doctor called because the baby was ill: before he arrived, her husband mentioned that he had not slept well. The doctor gave him a prescription.* MR LEVY *next asked about the knife which had been sharpened.* MRS HUME *said she did not know much about it. She was rather worried that day about the child, and was arranging for it to go into hospital the following day. She did not have any particular recollection about the knife being sharpened that day. She and her husband had lunch in the flat as usual that day, 5 October, but she was unable to remember what they had.*

MR LEVY: You knew very little about your husband's life or how he earned his money?—Very little.

On the afternoon of 5 October, did you know of three men going to the flat?—No.

During the whole of that morning, from 6 am, when you fed the baby, until you had lunch, do you think it would have been possible for your husband to have been cutting up the body of a man in that flat without your knowing anything about it?—No.

Did he in fact do anything of that sort to your knowledge? —(*The witness shook her head.*)

Did you, during the whole of that period, see the slightest sign of anything unusual such as I have suggested?—Nothing at all.

Did you see any signs of blood?—No.

Did you smell anything?—No.

Did you seen any bloodstained knives or anything?—I saw nothing.

MRS HUME *said that she went upstairs to feed the baby at two o'clock. She remembered Mrs Stride arriving, and soon afterwards she (Mrs Hume) went out with the baby as usual. She said that the saw which the police found in the flat when they were making inquiries was from a tool set she had given her husband; there was also a chopper and a carving-knife in the flat, which the police took away.*

Cross-examined by MR HUMPHREYS: You did not know much of your husband's private life, did you?—No.

He told you he was earning his living by flying planes?—Yes.

Did you know various parcels came to the flat on 5 and 6 October and were taken away by him?—No.

Did you know human blood in quantity was spilt in two or three different places?—No.

Did you know that three men came to the flat on 5 October? —No.

Did your husband give you any money that day?—He gave me £80, mostly in £5 notes.

Can you remember whether you had a coal fire the first week in October?—I don't know.

Do you remember what sort of a rug there was in the hall? —A normal rug—green, with a floral pattern.

Mrs Stride said that when she came to the flat it had gone. Do you remember what happened to it?—No.

Do you remember a party at the flat to celebrate the baby's arrival?—We did have some friends in.

Do you remember the carpet going to be dyed on 5 October?—Yes, there were stains all over it.

I am talking about one bad stain in the middle.

MR HUMPHREYS *asked for the carpet to be unrolled and held up for the witness's inspection.* MRS HUME *stared at it for a moment before saying to the Judge:* 'I am short-sighted.'

MR HUMPHREYS: Well, go down and look at it. (*After Mrs Hume had returned to the witness-box:*) You do not remember seeing that stain before 5 October?—Well, that is on the underside of the carpet.

Do you remember seeing the stain on the front of the carpet about the place where it now appears on the back?—I don't remember seeing it.

So far as you know, when the carpet came back from the cleaners it was put down in the same position as before?—I don't know.

How many times was the floor stained between September 1948, when you moved into the flat, and September 1949?—I don't know how many times, but I know it was more than once. My husband did it twice.

Do you remember if there was a joint for lunch on 5 October?—No.

Do you remember sending your husband out that day in a hurry to get a knife sharpened?—No.

You were never to your knowledge threatened by anybody about anything, were you?—Not to my knowledge.

MR LEVY (*to the Judge*) I understand that this lady is very desirous of making a statement regarding an incident that occurred in court on Friday. It is no part of my case, but she has asked me to mention it, and perhaps you will consider it.

MR JUSTICE SELLERS: I do not think it is necessary in such a trial. I do not think there is any prejudice against you at all, Mrs Hume. The Court has had an explanation from Mr Duncan Webb.

CYRIL JOHN LEE, *an ex-Artillery officer, said that to the best of his knowledge he had never met Hume. He had read*

reports of the trial and had got in touch with the Defence.
He knew Cambridge Terrace Mews very well, having lived
there between November 1946 and March 1949.

MR LEVY: Was there much activity at Mr Setty's garage in
the time you knew it?—I would say he did a brisk trade.

What was the nature of the work you saw done there?—
Repair work.

Anything else?—A certain amount of spraying motor-cars.

What kind of people usually went there?—The sort of
people you expect to take cars in for repairs—mostly local
business people.

Any others?—Half-way through my stay there, a rather
different sort of people started to appear. Not the sort of
people I would like to see around my doorstep.

What sort of people?—I should say spivs.

Did they appear to be English or foreign?—A very mixed
bag.

Did you hear the names Green, Mac or The Boy in
connection with Setty's garage?—To be very precise about it,
I did hear two of these names called out in the mews outside
my flat.

Was your mews near the garage?—Yes, it is a short mews,
about one hundred feet long and thirty feet wide. I did hear
the names Maxie and The Boy.

In what way did you hear them?—Somebody called out to
them.

So far as these two men are concerned, did you notice the
persons to whom the names were addressed?—No.

So you are not able to give us a description of these two?—
No.

Have you seen in the newspapers a more detailed description by which Hume has described the man Green?—I've
seen it, but not in the newspapers.

Did you ever see anyone in that mews of that description?—
Yes, on one occasion.

Did you hear any name or address which you could attach
to him?—No.

So you cannot tell us by what other name he was known?—
No, I cannot.

Cross-examined by MR HUMPHREYS: Would it be of any

use to you if I produced The Boy? There is in this court a man with that name, and his name is Baker?—I might recognise him as having been there.

A youngish, dark-haired man wearing a black overcoat was called, and stood for a moment facing the Judge.

MR HUMPHREYS: Have you ever seen him before?—No.

Do you know that Setty's brother has another garage next door in the same mews, and that he is called Max?—No.

ALFRED PERCY HARRY SPENCER, *of 620 Finchley Road, said that he was a headmaster and lived in the flat below Mr and Mrs Hume. On 4 October he was at home from 5.10 to 10.30 pm, when he went to bed. During that time he did not hear any unusual sounds from the flat above.*

Cross-examined by MR HUMPHREYS: You were sitting in a room which was really underneath the large coal cupboard in Hume's flat. Geographically, your flat is not quite the same as the one above?—Yes, I was sitting partly underneath the coal cupboard. The flat is not quite the same.

Can you hear people moving about in Hume's flat at all?— If the carpet is down, I should say not.

Did you hear people moving about on that night?—No, not more than usual.

MR JUSTICE SELLERS: What have you in fact heard?—The only thing we have heard is when they have been into the cupboard to get coal.

MR HUMPHREYS: Did you hear, for instance, on the night of the 5th, anything particular, as of a very heavy weight being put into the coal-hole?—No.

STANLEY HUSSEY, *of Ealing, a mechanic at Saunders' garage, said that he often saw Hume at the garage.* MR LEVY *handed him a carving-knife and the witness said he had sharpened it for Hume on 15 June last; it had the appearance of having been ground before.*

DR KEITH BLATCHLEY, *police divisional surgeon, said that in the autumn of 1949 he was attending Mrs Hume and her baby. He saw Hume on 3 October and received from him £30 in £5 notes. He had been pressing Hume for the money. Later he handed the notes to the police. On the morning of 5 October he saw Mrs Hume and, after attending to her baby, washed his hands in the bathroom. He noticed nothing unusual in any part of the flat that he went into. He found no signs of blood in the bathroom. He gave Hume a prescription for sleeping tablets.*

DR ROBERT DONALD TEARE, *pathologist, said that in sudden or violent death the blood became very fluid, losing its power to clot. The time was variable, but generally speaking it took ninety minutes after death for blood to lose its power of coagulation, and then it would remain fluid. It would dry like any other fluid, but it would not coagulate. He had examined the floorboards at Hume's flat, which he had first visited on 15 December. At that time, some floorboards from the dining-room had been taken away, and he saw floorboards which had been put in their place.*

MR LEVY: As far as the others were concerned, those that were not taken up, did you notice if there were any spaces between the boards?—Yes, there were gaps between the boards

Would blood of the sort of which you have told us pass between spaces of that kind?—Yes, it would.

I just want to ask you about quantities of blood. On the assumption that Setty weighed 13½ stone, what do you say would be the quantity of blood in his body?—I agree with Dr Camps that it would vary between fairly wide limits, but I should expect a body of that weight to have approximately 13 pints of blood.

And how much of that would you expect to remain in the torso if the head and legs were detached?—I should say approximately between 8 and 10 pints.

Where the body received stab wounds, would a certain amount have escaped from those wounds?—Possibly not: in all probability, not a great deal.

What would be the immediate effect of stab wounds of that kind, so far as blood is concerned? Would you expect a spurting of blood from the wounds?—Not necessarily, no.

Or a seeping from them?—Yes, I should expect that.

And in that way there would be a loss of blood, would there?—Yes.

Would there be a loss of very much blood in that way?—I would not expect more than would soak the clothing of the breast. From the type of wound that Dr Camps has described,

I should expect that there would be a considerable amount of coughing up of blood.

Would that be immediate?—Yes, or within a few seconds. It would come out as a very violent cough.

I want your views as to the probable consequences of a frontal attack by stabbing upon a man like Setty by a single assailant. It has been said by Dr Camps, I think, that it is conceivable that the whole thing might pass off very quietly without struggle or noise of any kind. Would you expect that?—No, I should not.

What would you expect?—I would expect either considerable resistance on the part of the attacked man, resulting in all probability in injuries to his body in the way of defence or protective injuries to hand or arm; or I should expect a volume of blood to be coughed up which would be distributed over the assailant and adjacent structures such as walls or furniture—and the floor, of course.

Would you expect a person stabbed like that to be in a condition in which he could fight back or struggle?—I think he would have some time and some power with which to fight back.

Would you expect him to remain silent?—That I cannot answer.

On the other hand, if he were restrained by one or more persons from behind, Dr Camps has given it as his view that it could not have been done without leaving bruise marks where the restraint had been applied. What do you say about that?—A man could be restrained from behind without any bruise marks developing.

Suppose the torso were wrapped up in a parcel and moved about, I suppose some of the blood would seep out from the torso?—Yes, not only from the cut ends, but also it would tend to leak out of the stab wounds in the chest.

Suppose such a parcel with the torso were dropped in the way Hume said he dropped this one, what result would you expect from that?—I should expect that the impact with the floor would squeeze blood out of the folds in almost every direction.

Do you think it probable from these wounds that he was killed by one single assailant?—(*The witness paused for some time.*)

MR JUSTICE SELLERS: Do you regard this as a medical question?—I think that the absence of marks of defence upon the body renders it more likely that he was killed by more than one person.

DR TEARE *went on to say that he examined a number of floorboards from the cupboard in the kitchen. Marks or stains on them proved to be of human blood, group O. They were spread in a patch over three boards. He found a number of fibres on the boards similar to the felt round the torso.*

MR LEVY: I suppose you have a great deal of experience in cutting up human bones?—Yes.

Is it a very quiet process, sawing up human bones?—No, it is not. It produces a noise which drowns ordinary conversation. It is impossible to dictate to one's secretary while bodies are being sawn.

Would you expect the noise to be heard in the room below in an ordinary house?—Yes.

How long do you think it would take a person inexperienced in sawing human bones to saw across the thigh of a man of Setty's size?—I think it would take more than a minute.

Cross-examined by MR HUMPHREYS, *the witness agreed that it was more and more hard to dogmatise on clotting, because of recent discoveries.*

If a man is stabbed close to the middle of the chest, he is going to cough almost immediately a lot of blood, isn't he?—Yes.

If there was any bruising, it would certainly show after death, wouldn't it?—Yes.

You say you usually find that a man puts his hands up to defend himself, in which case he may get cut with the assailant's knife. Is that it?—Yes.

But suppose the assailant is holding him off with a pretty strong left arm, he can't do much, can he?—No.

In this case there was a $13\frac{1}{2}$-stone man, 5ft 6in in height, and very fat. Assuming a man in the forties, fat or very fat, is struck a violent blow in the chest, which in fact is a knife going deep into him, it is practically going to knock him out, isn't it, as far as being an assailant and fighting back is concerned?—No, I don't think so.

Do you know that his stomach was found to contain a great deal of alcohol?—It's the first time.

SIXTH DAY *Wednesday, 25 January*

MR LEVY *called a final witness for the Defence, telling the Judge*: 'This witness was not available to us until late last night, and came to us through channels we knew nothing about.'

DOUGLAS CLAY, *a writer, of Gloucester Avenue, NW, examined by* MR DUVEEN:

Where were you last year?—On 23 February I went to Paris.

And how long were you in Paris?—I returned at the end of August last year.

While you were in Paris, did you associate with anybody?—I met a number of people there who were part of a gang: they were engaged in the smuggling of arms to Palestine and cars to this country.

Were there two members of the gang who particularly attracted your attention?—There were two members of that gang who were employed on general duties, but generally strong-arm work, who were known as The Boy and Maxie.

MR DUVEEN *asked the witness what he had done with the information he had collected about the gang, and he replied that he had given it to the International Surêté and to the British Embassy in Paris. A few days ago he had telephoned Scotland Yard and had later been interviewed by three detectives. He had then contacted the Defence.*

Cross-examined by MR HUMPHREYS: How did you get in touch with this gang?—I met a man in a night-club in Paris, and I had to cash some travellers' cheques. When I went back with him to his hotel, he was arrested by the police, and the mere fact that I was present at his arrest and heard certain things he said gave me an *entrée* to this organisation.

You would agree that Maxie is a very well-known name?—Yes. There was one very famous Max in Paris at that time, and I asked them if they meant the famous Max.

So you saw a second Max in the same organisation?—Yes.

Re-examined by MR LEVY: Did the second Max correspond with the description you have given us?—No, not in any way. Not even by age.

CLOSING SPEECH ON BEHALF OF THE ACCUSED

MR LEVY: *said that the matter for the jury's consideration*

F

was the question of whether or not Hume was a truthful man.
At the outset and on his behalf, I have always admitted Hume
is not an angel. He is capable of telling a lie occasionally if it
suits him. He says 'I am not always truthful, but I am not a
murderer.' MR LEVY *submitted that the picture drawn by the
Prosecution of Hume's financial stress had been dispelled.
During the nine months before this occurrence, nearly £2,000
had passed through his account. His financial position could
not have been one that caused him very serious concern. He
paid his doctor £30 the day before Setty disappeared.* A man
who is desperately hard up does not pay his doctor over £30.

*The jury had to decide whether Hume murdered Setty at
the flat and cut up his body. The two went together: there
was no possibility that Hume could have murdered Setty anywhere else and then brought the body to the flat to be cut
up.* You have seen the staircase. No man could walk up that
staircase with a 13½-stone corpse on his shoulder and take it
into the flat, and indeed it is not suggested. The suggestion is
that he was brought alive to that flat on the evening of 4
October and there done to death, the body cut up and dumped
into the sea. *It had been suggested that no such persons as
Green, Mac and The Boy ever existed. Mr Mansfield and
Mr Salvadori had said that they did not know these people.*
Does it strike you as being a little strange that you are asked
to say, because two people, even if they were honest people,
did not know these three men, therefore they don't exist?
Fortunately, this case has received a great deal of publicity.
It has, by reason of that publicity, come to the notice of the
Defence that there are people who, in fact, have seen such
people and have known of the existence of such persons—
perhaps who are capable of violent and unlawful acts, and
even, perhaps, of murder. MR LEVY *recalled the evidence of
Douglas Clay, and asked*: In the light of that sort of evidence,
can you for a moment accept the fact that all these three men
never existed and are a product of the fertile imagination of
Mr Hume?

It has been said there were smears of blood on the first two
or three boards just in the doorway of the sitting-room, and
Hume has said he did not go into the sitting-room. I wonder
what is the value of that? It is clear that if there were blood

being smeared, some would inevitably be brought up on the soles of his shoes, and do you think he could say with certainty that he did not go into the sitting-room? If this man was dead in the drawing-room, you would have had more than a mere smear of blood at the doorway. You would have had blood coughed up in quantities that would have spread over the floor and would have spread between the boards. But there is no suggestion of that at all.

You are to suppose that he had decided he was going to murder this man, decided he was going to cut him up and dispose of his body by the use of a plane. Do you think that it would have occurred to anybody but a madman to take a man there for the purpose of murdering him and cutting him up, knowing that at any time he might be interrupted by his wife—a gentle little woman, as you could see—who, like any other woman, would immediately go into hysterics and scream the place down? Mrs Hume is as honest a witness as you could ever have seen. Do you think that anybody but an absolute madman would contemplate doing a thing of that sort? On the other hand it would be easy for a gang to cut up this man and take the body to Hume for him to dispose of. That would be comparatively easy and with no undue risk, because these people, presumably, have at their disposal places which are more convenient for the purpose of murder and cutting up than Mr Hume's flat. There can be no doubt at all on which side the balance comes down.

Dr Donald Teare, an eminent pathologist—and his evidence might have commended itself to you because you remember how extremely cautious and reticent he was about this matter —said that if the man were attacked by a single man endeavouring to stab him, there would, in his view, have been a struggle and that blood would have spurted out from his mouth. He thought that the attacked man's arms would have gone up to protect himself, to clutch at the knife, and that there would have been, in all probability, the noise of a struggle.

Do you think Hume would go to the front of the man and stab him in his chest, or do you think he would seek opportunity, which he must have had, of going round behind him and burying his knife between his shoulder-blades? There can be no possible reasonable doubt that the man who died from those stab wounds in the chest was being held and restrained from behind. The chances of its having been done from the front by one man are so remote that you can dismiss them as being absurd. I submit that that man was murdered not by one man but by several. And there you have Mac, The Boy and Green—not a question of finding an alternative to Hume, but of finding a number of men.

MR LEVY *referred to the stained carpet in the sitting-room:* Was that stain made while the carpet was down, lying upon the underfelt? Could blood have got in such quantities to the underbinding of that carpet as to make it still apparent even after the rigours of cleaning and dyeing, and then make not the slightest mark on the underfelt beneath it? There was ample opportunity for the carpet to have gathered up all sorts of things, even bloodstains, in its journeyings, from the time it left the flat until it returned.

Dealing with Mrs Hume's evidence, MR LEVY *said:* It is quite impossible that Mrs Hume could have been in that flat all the time she was and be entirely ignorant of the sort of goings-on that the Prosecution suggest were taking place. Therefore I ask you to reject without the slightest hesitation the whole theory that this man could have been murdered by Hume in that flat in the way the Prosecution suggest.

CLOSING SPEECH FOR THE PROSECUTION

MR HUMPHREYS: The charge against this man is not carefully premeditated murder. It is no part of my duty to say that Setty was lured to this flat and there deliberately murdered by a man who intended to murder him. For all I know it may have been a chance quarrel, it may have been a dispute arising upon some contract, upon some business they were doing together; they may both have been drunk. I don't have to prove why that murder took place. It has never been the case of the Prosecution that Hume must necessarily have alone murdered Setty. He may have brought some other man to the flat with him. Some other man may have been waiting when Hume brought Setty back. It matters not, according to the law of England, whether or not Setty was alone. May I make it clear at once? It is not the duty of the Prosecution to get a conviction; it is the duty of the Prosecution to place the whole of the facts, so far as we know them, before the court.

MR HUMPHREYS *said that* MR LEVY *had addressed the jury on Mrs Hume at all times on the assumption that if they were satisfied that she must have known that a certain thing was happening in the flat, and that thing was too terrible to be contemplated, therefore it did not happen.* I am not prosecuting Mrs Hume; I am not defending her. She is first and foremost the wife of the man she loves. There is a law older than the law of England or any man-made law: a man and wife who love one another stick together. I do not say that Mrs Hume had no part in this murder; I say I have no evidence whatsoever that she had any part in it. I certainly do not agree necessarily that she had no part in the cutting up of the body and the tidying-up of the flat. That is entirely a matter for you to consider.

May I put this case before you as a picture in which there are three groups of evidence? One is the final piece in the jigsaw puzzle—are you satisfied that Hume murdered Setty? Two, was he murdered in Hume's flat and there cut up? And three is concerning the disposition of the remains.

You know the answer to point three, don't you? Do you doubt for one moment, after you heard Hume cross-examined, that Hume knew perfectly well that he was disposing of the murdered remains of Setty? He has almost said so in his written statement. Yesterday, under cross-examination, were you left in any doubt that that is what he knew, at least on the second trip with a big bloody parcel which spurted blood, when he knew that Setty was missing? I shall say no more about the whole of that part of the case. I shall assume you are satisfied that Hume has virtually confessed to disposing of the murdered remains of some man, and it was obviously Setty.

If Hume was also the man in whose flat Setty was murdered and cut up, would you have any doubt at all that Hume was the murderer, or was present and party to the murder and the cutting up? If, on the other hand, you are not satisfied that the body was cut up in the flat and the murder there took place, then the case for the Prosecution is substantially weakened. But if you are satisfied that you can add number two to number three, which you know, have you any doubt whatsoever that Hume is guilty and that you have the solution to number one?

Referring to Mac, Green and The Boy, MR HUMPHREYS *said:* I hope I have never said these three men did not exist in the sense that no such persons walking the earth bear those descriptions. Of course, there are people called Green and Mac and, of course, people called Boy. I asked you to believe that his story of the three men coming to him and tempting him to dispose of some crime of theirs and bringing him parcels and asking him to dispose of them, is a complete fabrication, and I still ask you to say so.

I suggest that Hume's account of the events of 5 October was a most amazing series of coincidences which you think was utterly beyond belief. First of all, for the first time in his life, he suddenly decides to have the carpet cleaned. On that day he suddenly decides to rush around the corner to get a knife sharpened, and cannot wait for it to be properly sharpened; and of all days in his life, he suddenly decides on that day to spend an hour in the kitchen—where he must not be disturbed because he is clearing out a coal cupboard. And of all times in his life and on the very next day, he has the floor stained. MR HUMPHREYS *then asked the jury if they thought that more than the whole of Setty's remains could not go in the parcels mentioned*: You may think other things went away, including the knife and saw and any clothes which had been bloodstained.

The case for the Defence was that a bloody parcel was put in the coal cupboard in Hume's flat; the case for the Prosecution was that a body was put in there. The murder, I suggest, took place the evening before. The body was cut up very rapidly thereafter. There was a whole night for that to be done. How does it help the Defence to account for every minute of the following day?

Finally, we come to Mrs Hume. Do you think she would fail to support and help her husband to the hilt in the terrible crisis which arose? Don't you think she would have done as she was told? What were the facts again? They are that she never saw three men come to the flat, that she never heard the bell, that she never saw any parcel anywhere, and that she never saw any blood.

One good point for the Defence is that no blood was found on the felt under the carpet where the blood fell on it. But the carpet has a thick pile which would take time for blood to soak through. Do you think it necessary that the cord on the back of the carpet was so stained that it must have left another stain on the felt underneath?

The absurdity of Hume's keeping Mrs Stride out of the kitchen while he turned out the coal cupboard and then looked through some insurance papers struck even him when he was in the witness-box; it produced what you may think was the crowning lie of the case—that he put on white shorts in order to clean out the coal cupboard. They did not meet very well in front and he was rather bashful about Mrs Stride seeing them. That you may think, is the lowest depths of lying in the witness-box. What was he doing in the kitchen for fifty minutes? Not cutting up Setty—that had been done the night before, shortly after death—but parcelling up little parts of Setty; that would take time. Sure enough, when he comes out fifty minutes later from his work, he has two parcels with him and off he goes.

If you add to the fact that Setty's body was obviously cut up in the flat, so was obviously murdered there, the fact that this self-confessed criminal, self-confessed liar admitted that he got rid of the murdered man's remains, do you want further proof that he was party to the murder? I have to prove no more.

THE SUMMING-UP

MR JUSTICE SELLERS *told the jury*: The difficulty of the case is that the Prosecution are not in a position to bring before you direct evidence which proves the charge which is alleged.

What they are seeking to do is to establish certain facts before you, and on those facts, if you find them proved, they ask you to say they point conclusively to the guilt of the defendant of the crime with which he is charged. But a further difficulty in the case is this: they allege that the evidence which has been given by Hume is invented and is deliberately untrue—a story which the man has invented as it was required in order to explain away, as best he could, the evidence which points against him, and on which the Crown asks you to come to the conclusion of guilt.

Hume says that his story, remarkable though it is, is true, and it does explain, he says, many of the matters which without an explanation might have led strongly to a conclusion of guilt. In this trial, as in all trials, we must ensure as best we can that an innocent man is not found guilty; but in the administration of justice it is desirable that a guilty man should not be acquitted because of skilful and sustained lying. You have to see whether there is any deliberate lying to cloak the truth, or whether you can accept Hume's story and thereby find many answers to the problems which confront you.

The matter for your consideration is: 'Has it been proved that Hume inflicted the stab wounds in Setty's body?' You may think there is no question that Setty was deliberately murdered. The question is, how does the evidence stand, as alleged against Hume, that Hume was responsible for the murder? The Prosecution submit to you that if they proved that Hume cut up the body, he was probably the murderer, and if they go on to prove, as seems to be admitted, that he disposed of the body, they say that very probably the person who disposed of the body is the murderer. The Prosecution have put the two together, and say that you will have no difficulty in arriving at the conclusion that Hume was the murderer, either alone or possibly in conjunction with someone else.

What is a vital date in this case? Is it not 4 October? It may have struck you, and struck very forcibly, that although one has had evidence of 30 September and the intervening days, perhaps 1, 2 and 3 October, and again of 5 and 6 October, about the activities of Hume, what evidence is there from him or any other witness as to what Hume did on 4 October? When Hume was asked to account for his movements on 4 and 5 October, the answer the police officers said he gave was 'that's going to be difficult'. Well, what evidence have we now, after this trial, of the movements of Hume on that vital day? There were some suggestions made by the prisoner when he gave evidence that the statement which he made—a long one—was not fair. It was not always in his own language, he said; it was sometimes in police language, and it was not read over. If you think that there is anything which makes the statement unfair, so that the prisoner is at some disadvantage, or saying something which he did not intend to say or might not be accurate, then, members of the jury, disregard it. Make a safe rule: disregard it entirely. If, on the other hand, you think it was what he was intending to say at the time, be it right or wrong, and the officer in charge accurately took it down, and that the superintendent who was inquiring was being fair and proper and within bounds, then you may attach importance to it.

MR JUSTICE SELLERS *said that Hume's evidence was that he had slept with his wife in the ordinary way on the Tuesday, 4 October. Mrs Hume, asked about Tuesday, 4 October, said that she listened to a programme on the wireless, but she did not say at that time that her husband was with her, and the implication was rather that he was not.* 4 October is, as far as evidence relating to Hume is concerned, practically a blank, and you may ask yourselves why that is so. Indeed, not a word was produced from morning to night as to his activities. You know something of Setty's movements from witnesses called, but nothing after 5.50 pm. You know nothing also about Hume's, not only up to 5.50 but prior to 5.50—not, at any rate, until late at night, when Mrs Hume said that as far as she could remember he went to bed with her in the ordinary way.

At one o'clock—apparently a most inconvenient time—on 5 October, the prisoner is said by a man named Edwards to have gone across to a garage to have a knife sharpened. There was some evidence that he was in a hurry and had it sharpened with a grindstone and not finished off with an oilstone, to leave it with a keen edge but not one which would last very long. You will have to ask yourselves—why go across at that time to have a knife sharpened?—realising that each of these matters may have quite an innocent explanation. You have to decide whether you accept them. On the other hand, you may think that they fit in with another aspect of the case which has not an innocent explanation.

If on the night before, or during the night, there had been something happening in the flat which marked the drawing-room carpet and stained it with blood, it might have been by someone who did not want it to be known, and who would deem it desirable to have the carpet cleaned at the quickest possible moment. If something had happened the night before which had either blunted the carving-knife or made it necessary or desirable to have a sharp knife, then that might be the reason for having the knife sharpened at one o'clock on that particular day.

It is not always that you have a witness who assesses his own honesty, but in this case Hume has ventured to set before you his own standard of honesty. You need not accept that, and can, if you like, think him more honest than he says or you can think him less honest than he says. You remember he used a curious phrase and said he was 'semi-honest'. If you accept that—whatever it may be—you may say, where his evidence is in conflict with somebody else's, that you prefer the other person's who seems more honest or really honest. As we go along you have to make up your minds whether you can accept Hume's evidence as correct. If you think he is a dishonest man and readily tells lies or romances, and if he is prepared to say anything which will fit the occasion, you will have to be very cautious and finally make up your minds whether you believe it or not. If you think he is deliberately lying, you may ask yourselves why does he do that if there is an innocent explanation, one which could be made without lying. You will have to deal with that.

If you come to the conclusion that the two parcels alleged to have been taken from the flat by Hume on the afternoon of 5 October were parts of the body of Setty, you will ask yourselves when they came into the flat, how they came there and how they came in that condition, severed from the body. At 4.10, or thereabouts, Hume goes out with two parcels. About five o'clock he arrived, if you accept the evidence of Mr Davey, at Elstree aerodrome with two parcels. He took an aeroplane and flew away.

SEVENTH DAY *Thursday, 26 January*

THE SUMMING-UP (*continued*)

MR JUSTICE SELLERS *again drew the attention of the jury to the lack of evidence with regard to the activities of Hume on 4 October. He went on*: About the next day Hume has given a great deal of evidence. It is not for Hume to prove himself innocent, and indeed it is not necessary for him to give any evidence at all; it is for the prosecution to prove his guilt. He has given evidence in the witness-box. He has not told of his movements on that vital day, 4 October. He did say he had not seen Setty that day—because, you will remember, he said he had not seen Setty for two years. MR JUSTICE SELLERS *said the jury had to fit the fact of the absence of assistance regarding 4 October into their assessment of the whole story.* As you approach the consideration of Wednesday you have to remember that, overnight, 4–5 October, Setty would appear to have disappeared.

The evidence of the prosecution established certain events happening in or around Hume and his flat, starting from 10 am on 5 October. *Hume deposited £90 in his bank against an overdraft of £78. He visited the cleaners with the sitting-room carpet and took the knife to be sharpened at 1 pm. There was the evidence of Mrs Stride of Hume's departure with two parcels, and evidence of his flying from Elstree with the parcels and arriving at Southend without them.* You will have to consider this very carefully and decide whether or not this evidence, standing alone, points to the implication of Hume in the death of Stanley Setty. If after the investigation of Hume's evidence, you reject it, you are left with these circumstances, with one added piece of evidence. It is that in Hume's flat there was found evidence of human blood of group O, the same group as Stanley Setty's. This does not mean that it is essentially Setty's, because some 40 per cent of the population—it may be more than that—has that group of blood.

MR JUSTICE SELLERS *referred to Hume's statement to the police on 26 October*: Does it not seem to say this—the two packages which arrived on Wednesday were dry—that is, no blood was coming from them, they were free from stains. The third package, which came on Wednesday night, was carried by two of the men, he says, and put in the cupboard. In that statement there does not appear to be any indication that the package was put down in the dining-room or anywhere other than in the cupboard, and there is no reference to the fact that it was being brought out, was being dropped down in the dining-room, or was dragged in the hall. That is important because you have a fuller, and you may think a different statement from Hume in the witness-box. And what you have to deal with is the bloodstains, which you may think have been proved to have been found in the flat. You have to consider where they were found, whether they were to your complete satisfaction bloodstains, and then—how did they come about? Did they come about because there was the murder of Setty in the flat, or by the blood being dripped from one of the parcels? Hume's statement said that the parcel was put into the coal cupboard, and his evidence said that it was put down in the dining-room in the afternoon and left a pool of blood which he cleared up.

The important thing is the evidence he gives about those three men going that afternoon and again in the evening to the flat, bringing on one occasion two parcels, and on the other, one. Can you find anywhere in any of the evidence of this case any support for this? Whatever view you take, something unusual was happening in the flat that day. Mrs Hume was apparently there all day. She went out, as was customary with the baby. If the two parcels came there, she knew nothing of them, and if blood were spilled on the dining-room floor or elsewhere she made no reference to it. With regard to the call of the three men, there is no corroboration from Mr Hume or Mrs Stride.

Hume has asked you to accept a story—I might say an improbable story (of course, improbable stories do happen)— that in broad daylight, between two and three o'clock in the afternoon, three men brought two parcels to his flat. You may think they were the limbs of the dead man, Setty. If those three men, you may think, had not committed the murder then they knew something about it. You have to consider this story, which involves three men bringing parcels along a busy road to Hume's flat. You have to consider how much they knew of Hume—how much they could trust him. All this came out of a casual meeting on 3 September. You know that Hume lived in the flat with his wife and young child. How were the three men to know that his wife would not be there? Was it not a grave risk for these three men to carry the parcels up to the flat to place them in the care of a man they had no reason to trust

According to the statement, in the evening—not very late evening—of the 5th, there was a car with three men and the torso of the murdered man inside, in a road opposite the flat. Two men were sitting inside the car and the third man was waiting at about 8.45 by the bus stop for Hume. A grave risk, you may think, for them to take. Then they had to take the parcels to the flat, with the possibility of Mrs Hume being there. She might have told the police.

You have to consider the blood on the dining-room floor. Hume did not tell the police. Mac, or Maxie, Greeny and The Boy had gone. What were they to him? All he says is that in the afternoon one of them pointed a revolver at him. You have to consider from that point of view whether it is a credible story. If you accept that story, then the verdict you must return is not guilty. If there is any doubt in your mind about it, then you also have to return a verdict of not guilty. If you reject that story entirely and say it is false and put it on one side, then you must consider the other evidence. You have to consider the story of the three men named Mac, or Maxie, Greeny and The Boy. You will have to ask yourselves: 'Are these three men, for the purpose of Hume, an invention?' Suppose he were inventing these things and these men. It is perhaps reasonable that he might choose those names. They are not unfamiliar names in a certain society. It is not difficult to invent names, neither is it difficult to invent descriptions. The fact is that neither the police inquiries nor the prisoner nor the efforts of those assisting him nor the publicity which this case has been given has resulted in any one of those three being brought before you. Mr Lee, who lived in the mews where Setty had a garage, says he remembers hearing two names being called out beneath his windows; he remembers on another occasion seeing another man whose description might be that of a man described by Hume. You have the story of Clay, who says he is a writer, and who in some ways became associated with some gang or other in Paris; he told you of two men he met in Paris, called Max and The Boy.

Are you satisfied that these three men are the three men who called at that flat in Finchley Road, in those terrible circumstances, bringing the dismembered body of a man who must have been murdered some time after 5.50 pm on 4

October? No names or addresses—the story was that they departed in the afternoon still owing £50, with the prisoner not knowing whether they would return or no. That, I think, is the line of inquiry to which I invite you, along with anything else you think can test the evidence in this case.

You may think that the sitting-room carpet becomes one of the most important pieces of evidence in this case. You have to make up your mind whether it has been proved that the sitting-room carpet was before—and immediately before, some time within the previous twenty-four hours—taken away to be cleaned because it was freshly stained with blood. That is a most important decision for you to make. If you find that it was, then you have to fit that in with the other evidence, and that may throw some further light on your assessment of the reliability of Hume's story. You will remember that he has not said that any one of those packages was ever brought into the sitting-room. You must ask, is that all the blood there was, or was there blood in the sitting-room? You must decide if there was blood in the sitting-room, not just trodden in so that faint traces appeared on the boards, but a substantial quantity of blood on the sitting-room carpet. If you reject any blood in the sitting-room, you have in the evidence of Hume an explanation of how the blood might have got into the cupboard, the dining-room and the hall. If you accept the bloodstains on the sitting-room carpet, and you think it happened immediately before the carpet was taken to the cleaners, what explanation have you from Hume as to how it got there?

There was no bruising on the torso. Do you think this attack could have been made by Hume in the front without any sign of injury to the assailed man—other signs, that is, which might be regarded as defence wounds to hands and arms, or something like that? All that is known is of direct blows on the chest.

Then it is said there were no signs of injury on Hume, or of bloodstains on his clothing. No one, perhaps, is in a position to say precisely what was done. What you have to conclude is whether you can, with certainty, say that that attack must have taken place in this flat, in all probability in that room, and that it was done by the hand of Hume.

Speaking of the motive for the murder, MR JUSTICE SELLERS *said*: Is it not possible some quarrel cropped up? You may think, if you do not accept the monetary lure as a motive, that no motive has been provided with regard to a quarrel or anything else. On the other hand, you may think that in all the circumstances, there may have been many motives of which we know nothing.

If you reject Hume's evidence entirely, or you reject it as even so doubtful that you can disregard it altogether, you will still have this question: Did all the matters the Prosecution have spoken about actually happen?

The jury retired at 12.30 pm and returned at 3.02 pm.

FAILURE TO AGREE; SECOND INDICTMENT

THE CLERK OF THE COURT: Members of the jury, will your foreman please stand? Mr Foreman of the jury, are you agreed upon your verdict?

THE FOREMAN: My Lord, we are not agreed. I feel that it is doubtful that we shall reach a unanimous decision.

MR JUSTICE SELLERS: Then I have no other course but to discharge you, with the thanks of the City for your long and strenuous service.

MR HUMPHREYS *said that the possibility of a disagreement had occurred to him and he had taken instructions from the Director of Public Prosecutions (Sir Theobald Mathew), who was present in court, as to what was the right course to pursue. It was not necessarily in the interests of justice that there should be a retrial of the case.* I must respectfully ask that another jury be sworn in order that no evidence may be offered on this indictment, and thereafter to offer evidence on another indictment on the file.

A new jury, also of ten men and two women, were sworn. They were told that Hume was charged with the murder of Stanley Setty and that to that indictment he had pleaded Not Guilty. MR JUSTICE SELLERS *told the jury that the Prosecution offered no evidence against him, and directed the jury to return a verdict of Not Guilty of murder.*

THE CLERK OF THE COURT (*to Hume*): There is a second indictment, which charges you with being an accessory after the fact to murder, knowing that a certain person or persons unknown on 4 October 1949 murdered Stanley Setty, and that you on 5 or 6 October 1949 assisted and maintained that person or those persons by disposing of the body of the said Stanley Setty.

To that indictment HUME *pleaded Guilty.*

MR HUMPHREYS: Your Lordship is now in full possession of the facts of this case, and I have nothing to add.

MR LEVY: I feel I am entitled to ask you, my Lord, to assume in favour of Hume that at least a number of the members of the previous jury accepted his explanation of what happened.

MR JUSTICE SELLERS: I think I am bound to assume they did not reject it.

MR LEVY: In that case, it means this—that he first accepted from the men of whom he has spoken, two parcels, the contents of which he thought were comparatively innocent. These parcels were disposed of in a way my Lord has heard. At a later date he received a third parcel, and quite obviously must have come to the conclusion that it contained the remains of some human body, probably that of someone who had been murdered. At that time he was heavily involved in this matter. You will remember that on a previous occasion he had been shown a revolver. He was then, with the receiving of the third parcel, on the horns of a very grave dilemma. He knew that if he failed to carry out the orders, he was dealing with a gang of men who would not hesitate to murder, and that his life was, to some extent, in danger. It might be said that he could and should have communicated with the police. If he had done this his life would not have been worth a moment's grace. He found himself in an appalling position and felt he had no alternative.

MR JUSTICE SELLERS (*addressing Hume*): I find it hard to imagine a graver case. For no other reason than for money, £150, you were prepared to take part of the body, the torso, knowing what it was, and keep it in your flat overnight. Then, without any communication to the police, you took it away and flung it into the Thames estuary with the intention and belief that nothing more would be known of it, thereby obliterating all evidence of the crime of murder. The sentence of the Court upon you is twelve years' imprisonment.

THE CONFESSION

Brian Donald Hume was released from prison on 1 February 1958, having served his sentence at Wakefield and Dartmoor, earning the full remission for good conduct. It appears that he was well liked by his fellow-prisoners, who christened him The Fuse because of his knowledge of electrical work; he showed his friends how to make radio sets out of smuggled parts and pieces of Post Office equipment sent in for dismantling. When the time of his discharge arrived, a feast was set out on a ping-pong table, the focal point being a large iced cake, bearing the message 'A fuse will be blowing shortly' with a drawing in coloured icing of an aeroplane with a bundle dropping from it.

A meeting that appears to have made a strong impression on him during the years of imprisonment was that with Klaus Fuchs, the traitor. Hume expressed a warm admiration for him, and intended to renew the acquaintanceship when Fuchs was released. Events, however, were to take another turn.

While he was in prison, Cynthia Hume had obtained a divorce on the grounds of cruelty. The marriage was dissolved in 1951, and she subsequently married the reporter, Duncan Webb, who died not long afterwards from the effects of war wounds. On his release Hume received a piece of news that upset him: his dog Tony, seemingly the only living being for whom he felt a genuine, disinterested affection, had been put to sleep some time previously;* now, he said, he was on his own. He was also short of money. He obtained a job in a factory at Welwyn Garden City, but the prospects were not such as to interest a man like Hume to any degree.

---

*In his excessive devotion to a dog, Hume interestingly resembles Myra Hindley, whose insane fury at the death of her mongrel, Puppet, while it was being examined for the police by a veterinary surgeon, far exceeded any emotion she felt over the killing of young children. See *Celebrated Trials Series: The Trial of Ian Brady and Myra Hindley;* edited by Jonathan Goodman (David & Charles, 1973).

But he had a disposable asset: a story to tell. Almost as soon as he was released, he tried to interest the press in an account of his life in prison and his reminiscences of Klaus Fuchs. Nobody cared. Among those he approached, however, was a newspaperman he already knew, Fred Redman of the *Sunday Pictorial*. Mr Redman had already interviewed Hume in prison, and was convinced of his guilt in the matter of Setty's murder. He told Hume he would settle for nothing less than a full confession. It was a large, possibly a dangerous, decision for Hume to make, even though he was aware that, under the double-jeopardy rule, he could not again undergo trial for killing Setty.

Eventually he accepted the offer from the newspaper of £2,000 for the full story. In April 1958 he had changed his name by deed poll to Donald Brown; and during May, while staying at a hotel in Westcliff-on-Sea, he was interviewed over a period of three weeks by a *Sunday Pictorial* reporter, Victor Sims. The story of his 'Confession'—polished and pointed for dramatic reading, but essentially as he told it—ran in the paper through the month of June.

After an account of the hardships of his early life, he began the details of the crime with the incident of the kick aimed by Setty at his dog. 'Nobody could do that to my pet dog and get away with it.' He then claimed that he had heard stories that Setty was having secret meetings with his wife, and taking her out during the afternoons. 'I was fast getting the needle with Setty', he remarked.

At about 7.35 on the evening of 4 October 1949, as it was getting dark, Hume arrived home, having had a few drinks, and saw Setty's Citroën parked outside. He hurried upstairs and found Setty seated on the sofa in the living-room: 'Something snapped inside my head. I boiled with rage.'

He told Setty to get out of the flat. Setty refused. A furious quarrel developed, and Hume went out to the landing and grabbed a German SS dagger which hung with other souvenirs on the wall. 'Now,' he reported himself as thinking, 'those SS initials stood for forty-four-year-old Stanley Setty.' His declared intention was merely to frighten the other man, but he had reckoned without his own 'mad rage'. Setty taunted him with playing at soldiers and swung at him with the back of his hand. They grappled, and as they rolled on the floor Hume stabbed at him repeatedly in the chest and legs, at the same time trying to keep Setty away so as to avoid becoming bloodstained. Suddenly Setty slumped against the sofa and on to the floor. He began to cough, and rolled on his back. Hume looked at the clock, he said, and noted that the fight had lasted less than two minutes. 'The thought flashed through my mind that perhaps I could get away with murder.'

He grasped the heavy body by the legs and dragged it—taking care to keep it on its back—across the hall, through the dining-room and scullery and into the breakfast-room. (This presumably is the room generally referred to at the trial as the kitchen.) He lugged it into the coal cupboard and covered it with an old piece of felt. Then he tidied up the lounge, covering a splash of blood with an armchair. He washed the blood off the sofa, threw away a broken lamp-standard, then went down to Setty's car. There was no ignition key, so he hurried upstairs again, felt through the dead man's pockets, extracted his car key, put on a pair of gloves to avoid leaving fingerprints, returned to the street, and drove off. He left the car in Cambridge Garden Mews and was back home by about 10.45. After more tidying up he went to bed and lay there 'smoking endlessly'—with, it may be granted, some excuse, if a certain lack of consideration for his wife.

In the morning he took the carpet to the cleaners as stated, and tried once again to remove bloodstains and fingerprints. (No prints of Setty were found in the flat.) He explained that the reason bloodstains were later found on the edge of the carpet and on the floor but not on the underfelt was that, having cut off a strip of felt which was stained, he discovered he could stretch the rest of the felt to cover the space left by the piece he had removed.

He next bought a tin of dark varnish to stain the floor where he had washed it. The dog apparently took a keen interest in the proceedings, 'looking up at me quizzically'—the adverb is a piquant one. During the long chain-smoking night, Hume had formulated his plan. As soon as Mrs Hume had gone out with the baby, leaving him alone in the flat, he dragged the body from the coal cupboard and fetched the tools he needed—a hacksaw and a cheap lino knife. (This, of course, disagrees with the evidence given at the trial, which referred to Hume taking a carving knife to be sharpened on the morning of 5 October, needing it in such a hurry that he was unable to wait for the job to be properly completed. John Williams notes in his book that as this evidence was being given Hume frowned angrily, convinced that the witness had relied on a most inconveniently faulty memory: the incident referred to had occurred on another day altogether and was entirely innocent. It was, of course a strong point in the Prosecution's favour—but not, as it turned out, sufficiently so as to turn the balance towards a unanimous verdict of guilty.)

His implements ready, he then set about his grisly task. First he cut some of the clothing away, leaving a silk shirt, jacket, underpants, socks and shoes; then he started work with the hacksaw—knowing nothing about surgery and apparently unmoved by either horror or fear, other than that of taking too long. It was now one o'clock, and Mrs Stride, the daily help, was due at 2.30. The only time a shiver seems to have gone through him was when he caught sight of Setty's lifeless eyes staring at him; he covered them with a piece of rag.

The next task was to wrap up the remains. He made a parcel of the legs and most of the clothes, then put the head into a box that had contained tins of baked-beans, weighting it with pieces of rubble he brought in from the back yard. According to his own account it was only when he began to rip the jacket from the torso that he became aware of the large sum of money Setty had been carrying. It was suggested at the trial that robbery was a major motive for the crime, but if Hume is to be believed, it was merely an unexpected bonus. As it was, he had to destroy all but some £90 because the remainder was either bloodstained or had been torn by the dagger in the struggle. 'It broke my heart to burn the fivers,' he said, 'but it would have been better for me if I had burned the lot.' This last comment was an allusion to his failure to notice that the serial numbers were consecutive, and thus to realise that they probably came direct from a bank and would be easy to trace.

He first put the torso into a cabin trunk, but found the lid would not close. He therefore wrapped it in felt, then in a white blanket, roped it tightly, then put the whole lot into another blanket with some pieces of lead for weights, and left it in the coal cupboard. He then took the first two packages (containing the head and the legs) down to a hired self-drive car waiting in the street. It was just about 2.30, and he managed to get clear of the house before Mrs Stride arrived. (Here there is another important difference between the 'Confession' and evidence given at the trial: according to Mrs Stride, Hume was in the flat when she arrived, had asked her on no account to disturb him in the kitchen as he was clearing out the coal cupboard—in white shorts—had sent her out to buy a floor-cloth, had told her about the missing carpet, and had actually passed her on the way downstairs with his two parcels.)

Accompanied by the dog, Hume then drove to Elstree, approaching the airfield along the aptly sinister Dagger Lane. He 'drove cautiously . . . trying to avoid driving mistakes'. He had no wish to be picked up for some trivial traffic offence, with the two parcels in the back of his car. The events of the flight are described in greater detail than in his statement to the police, but with only minor variations such as a few inconsistencies in the timing.

Expecting to be back before long, he left the dog in the car and started off at 3 pm, with a maximum of three and a half hours' flying time in the Auster on a full tank. After setting his course for Southend, his professed destination, he turned south-west and flew over the Channel at about 2,000ft until he saw the outline of France and what he took to be one of the Channel Islands. There he dropped his two parcels overboard. 'I looked for a sign of them on the sea. There was none. They must have sunk like stones.'

He turned for home. By this time the weather, which had been bright and sunny, was deteriorating, and the daylight had begun to fade. He made quickly for Southend airport, and landed after having flown for a little over three hours. His purpose was to draw as much attention as possible to the fact that he, Brian Donald Hume, had indeed carried out his declared intention of flying to Southend—and by a lucky mischance his landing helped to ensure this, for he violated the circuit drill and landed full in the path of a four-engined plane. Leaving the Auster to be refuelled, he took a taxi into the town—paying the driver with one of Setty's £5 notes—and went for a stroll on the Pier. It was by now too late to take his plane back to Elstree (he had neither experience in, nor a licence for, night flying), so he made his way back to Finchley by taxi. 'It cost a lot,' he remarked, 'but I had fivers to spare that day.'

An additional anxiety, which is not referred to in the trial records, was the fact that he had been forced to leave Tony overnight in the hired car at Elstree. He telephoned the airport, asking them to give the dog a run, and arranged to pick up the car the following morning. He then retired—to bed, rather than to sleep—for the second night, with the dismembered body of the man he had murdered hidden in the coal cupboard.

His first action on the morning of 6 October was to arrange for a man to stain the floor in the living-room. He went to Elstree by chauffeur-driven car, to collect the dog and his own car. Back in the flat with Tony, he dragged the weighty parcel out of the cupboard and asked the man who was staining the floor if he would give him a hand to carry it downstairs, as described in his evidence at the trial. For well over an hour he left the torso in the car outside his flat while he attended to a number of final details.

At length, again accompanied by Tony, he drove to South-end and loaded the parcel into the waiting Auster. A mechanic, seeing him struggle with the cumbersome package, asked him what it contained. 'With a quick smile I replied, "Fish".' Refusing help from the willing, if understandably puzzled, mechanic, Hume wedged the parcel into the front seat. The dog jumped into the back seat, and the plane took off. It was about three o'clock. Once over the sea beyond Southend Pier, he followed much the same south-west route as the previous day. As he approached the first of the Channel Islands, he prepared to dump his parcel.

From this moment the luck—the really extraordinary luck, one may think—that had sustained him since he first thrust the dagger into Setty's body, began to fail. He found it impossible to shift the awkward bundle. After a frantic struggle, trying to open the plane door, battle against the slipstream, and cope with the weight and size of the parcel in the cramped space—to say nothing of controlling the furiously barking dog—he succeeded. 'Suddenly there was an enormous bang as the door whipped open and then slammed shut. The torso was gone.' A moment later he received a much greater shock. In his struggles to push the parcel out he had loosened the rope. The outer blanket, with the lead weights inside it, had broken loose and was flapping over his tail elevators. It must have been a terrifying moment. The cabin was filled with flying dirt, together with coal dust which the blanket had gathered up from the cupboard in the flat. Somehow he managed to free the tail-plane, and prepared to set off for Elstree. Before doing so, he looked down to the sea. The torso, covered only by the inner wrapping, was floating on the surface of the water. After a wild momentary idea of ditching the plane and tying the bundle to it so that they would sink together, he realised there was nothing more to be done. Understandably distracted, and with the weather again deteriorating, he lost his bearings on the homeward flight, and landed in a field which a farmer told him was near Faversham, in Kent. By this time it was too late to make for Elstree—and in any case he had insufficient fuel for such a distance. He eventually landed, at about 6.15, at Gravesend. The following day he picked up his car from Southend, and arranged for the plane to be returned to Elstree.

The appalling two days were over. He had done what he could, and, despite the final mishap, must have felt reasonably secure. Already, however, the torso of the man he had killed had started its slow, fatal journey up the Channel, round the coast of Kent, past the Hell-fire Corner of the recent war and the estuary of the Thames—to lonely Dengie Flats: where it might have remained undiscovered for long enough, had it not been for Mr Tiffin's decision to spend a part of his holiday wild-fowling.

With news of the discovery of the body, 'a million questions throbbed through my mind. Had I covered my tracks well enough? Would the police now come looking for me? What was I going to say to them if they did?'

One matter had to be taken care of at once: the bloodstained cabin-trunk into which he had tried to force Setty's torso.

> I took it along to the left-luggage office at Golders Green tube station. Then I did a strange and stupid thing. Any other torso murderer would have taken the receipt for the trunk, torn it up, and not bothered about it or the trunk again. But not me. It was one more indication of the foolish risks I took to make this murder complicated when it could have been so simple. I screwed the ticket up and hid it between some coloured wires in the telephone junction box in my flat. In point of fact, by the time the police found it I was already in jail.

The main part of Hume's 'Confession' concludes, in suitably dramatic style: MY VICTIM'S BODY HAD FOLLOWED ME HOME. The rest briefly describes his arrest, admits to the falsity of the story of Max, Greenie and The Boy, and confirms that their descriptions were indeed based on the investigating Scotland Yard officers—Mac on Superintendent Colin MacDougall, Greenie on Chief Inspector John Jamieson, and The Boy on Detective Sergeant Sutherland. It was a touch of bland effrontery for which, even in the shameful circumstances, it is difficult to resist a sneaking feeling of admiration.

INTERLUDE

Hume did not wait for his 'Confession' to appear in the newspaper before leaving the country: untouchable by law for the murder of Setty he might be, but he realised well enough that his position was likely to be none too comfortable once the truth was out. Though his new name of Donald Brown was his by deed poll, he now found himself another which he was to use without such legal niceties. With a forethought worthy of a better cause, he went to Somerset House—where on a former occasion he had discovered the confirmation of his illegitimacy—and searched for the name of a person whose age coincided with his own. He chose John Stephen Bird, which, he said, attracted him both because 'bird' was a slang term for time spent in prison, and because of its association with flight and freedom. He disguised himself, for Mr Bird, with smarmed-down hair, spectacles and a false moustache. The last item was the most reckless and easily penetrable of facial alterations, but he would need it only to carry him to and from his destinations. He already had a passport as Donald Brown, but now needed one for his new personality. For Hume this was a simple matter. He returned to a familiar thoroughfare, Finchley Road, to have the necessary photograph taken, then arranged the required signature on the back by using a home-made rubber stamp of a solicitor's office and forging a name over it. During this time he lived in Brompton Square under another alias, John F. Lea.

On Sunday, 25 May 1958, as John Stephen Bird, chemical engineer, he left Ringway Airport, Manchester, for Zurich with his £2,000 in banknotes in his hand-luggage, having successfully evaded the Customs. He checked in at the St Gotthard Hotel and the next day changed the money into dollars at several different banks. He was now Brian Donald Hume in appearance, but had assumed yet another identity— Johnny Bird, Canadian test pilot—a creation perhaps suggested by his successful Pan-American airman performance with the Torquay Carnival Queen. As this new and dashing character, he set out to enjoy the worldly pleasures of Zurich. Almost at once he had a fateful encounter. In a night club he met a girl in her late twenties, Trudi Sommer, who was divorced from her husband and ran a hairdressing establishment. According to his own account, he was so attracted by her that he told her the very same evening that he was madly in love with her and wanted to marry her. 'Trudi,' he said, 'her head spinning with wine, seemed wide-eyed with astonishment at my sudden proposal.'* A not unreasonable reaction. Even so, she seemed almost equally taken by the impulsive, carefree test pilot, and though she told him he could not marry her as fast as he flew his planes, they immediately started going around together.

Hume had already laid certain plans. The journey to Switzerland had been merely for the purpose of changing his smuggled money into dollars. He then intended to start a new life in Canada, and had in fact booked a passage. As a result of the meeting with Trudi Sommer, he put his journey off for a few days, then told her he had to leave on a dangerous mission but would return and marry her. As Johnny Bird in both name and appearance, he passed through the controls at Idlewild and Montreal.

After a week in Canada, he crossed into the United States, visiting San Francisco, Los Angeles and Hollywood. For days and nights he 'whooped it up'. He also considered the possibility of making extra money by holding up a Los Angeles pay-roll wagon, but had just sufficient sense to drop the idea after hearing that a group of more professional gunmen had just pulled off a major job by the same means, and the authorities would be on the watch.

Despite all these excitements, he found America a disappointment, and decided to return to Trudi Sommer, with whom he had kept up a regular correspondence. On 3 July 1959 he arrived back in Zurich, wearing his spectacles and moustache on the journey as before, and surprised her by appearing at the door of her shop grasping two dozen

---

*Unless otherwise stated, all direct quotations from Hume are taken from his second series of interviews with Victor Sims, published in the *Sunday Pictorial* in October/November 1959.

red roses. Their relationship resumed where it had left off.

By this time, however, his money was running out, and one night to his dismay he discovered that he had only £150 left. Something had to be done without delay, and he started to plan an ambitious series of bank robberies. He would work in European countries, with Switzerland as his base. His first port of call, where surely they would hardly expect him to turn up again, would be England. Explaining his trip to the trusting Trudi Sommer by telling her that he was doing some anti-Russian spying for the Americans, he booked his passage late in July. Ringing the changes on his aliases and appearances from Bird to Brown *en route,* he arrived in London and put up at a hotel in Baker Street.

The bank chosen for his first operation was the Midland in Boston Manor Road, at Brentford, on the western outskirts of London, and the date was Saturday, 2 August, the day before the Bank Holiday closure. During that morning he paid a brief preliminary call, pretending to want information on opening an account, and saying that he would look in again later when he had made up his mind. This step was taken to ensure that he would be admitted again without suspicion just before the building was closed. He then went to the Globe public house in Brentford, where he had a glass of beer and swallowed a couple of pep pills. At two minutes to twelve he returned to the bank. The cashier, a man named Frank Lewis, was waiting by the door, but recognised Hume and let him in, closing the door behind him. Instantly Hume drew a gun and called out, in the best Hollywood gangster tradition, 'This is a stick-up!' Lewis made an instinctive movement, and Hume immediately shot him. He said afterwards that he thought the man was going to throw an inkstand in his face. As Lewis fell to the floor, wounded in the stomach, Hume waved his gun at the rest of the staff, demanding money. Someone opened a tin box and poured out the £5 notes it contained. 'I hadn't seen anything like it since the day I cut up the body of Stanley Setty and found his pockets stuffed with bloodstained notes,' Hume said, 'but these fivers weren't stained with blood.' After grabbing as many as he could and stuffing them into a canvas bag, he demanded to know what the large safe contained, but was told that it held nothing but ledgers and papers. He made the staff tie one another up, finishing off the process himself, pulled the telephone wires from their sockets, and scooped up what loose cash he could see. He was, in fact, playing for time, because his plan hinged on an escape route by a certain train to Putney, thence to the Cromwell Road Air Terminal. The wounded man was groaning is pain, and one of the staff begged Hume to do something for him. He agreed to do so later.

'Then it was time for me to leave. I had a quick last look round. A pretty girl was lying there, tied up, with her skirt raised above her shapely knees. I pulled it down. A girl is entitled to her modesty, even if she is tied up in a bank.'

After picking up the cartridge from the floor, he left the bank and went to the station, where he telephoned for a doctor to be sent to the wounded man. In the Air Terminal lavatory he transformed himself from Donald Brown to John Stephen Bird, caught the boat train at Victoria, and returned to Switzerland and Trudi Sommer.

His haul from the robbery was about £1,300, but he was furious to learn the following morning that he had been duped. The large safe had, in fact, contained some £40,000 in cash. The official had outwitted him. 'I believed him,' said Hume, 'because I thought that people outside of prison walls generally told the truth!' Raging, he swore that one day he would get even: 'Nobody lies to Hume and gets away with it'.

Meanwhile problems were arising from his relationship with Trudi, who naturally wanted to know when he would be able to carry out his fervently declared intention to marry her. He started to take some preliminary steps, but an awkward situation arose when he went with Trudi to the Zurich Town Hall to discover what papers were necessary. He was asked to produce his passport (which represented, of course, Mr Bird in the photograph, whereas his present appearance was Mr Hume), and the official immediately pointed out that the photograph did not look much like him, and suggested he should get it renewed. Trudi Sommer's surprise was even greater than the official's, and she began, not unreasonably, to ask some awkward questions. According to Hume, from that time on suspicion and doubt were present in her mind.

It was time for more trips. He made one to Frankfurt, then again crossed to Canada. His plans appear to have been vague. John Williams states that his Canadian trip was intended to enable him to forget Trudi altogether. He could not do so, however. While in Canada he applied for papers to enable him to marry her, perjuring himself by the adoption of yet another characterisation—British-born John Bird, aviation engineer. He then returned to Switzerland and told the singularly patient and faithful Trudi that they would be married in February 1959.

By this time the cash from the Brentford raid was running out. In order to combine the pleasure of revenge with the business of robbery, he decided to take the considerable risk of attacking the same bank a second time. Following the usual personality procedure, he arrived in London on 4 November and went to a small hotel in Kensington. On the following day, wearing a pair of dark glasses, he went to revisit the bank, passing on the way a police poster offering a reward of £1,000 for information leading to the arrest of the man who had made the raid in August. 'It made me feel good to know I was wanted,' he said. But a shock soon deprived him of any such feeling: on arriving at Boston Manor Road he found that the bank had moved.

On the door was a notice giving the new address, a quarter of a mile or so away in the Great West Road. When he went there he found scaffolding erected against the building. Ever ingenious, he disguised himself as a workman and climbed up to look inside and familiarise himself with the layout. He went back to his hotel and waited until the afternoon of 12 November. The intervening days he spent improving his mind at museums and picture galleries—which also had the advantage, of course, of costing him nothing. At two minutes before closing time on the appointed day, he boldly entered the bank, waving his gun and shouting as before: 'This is a stick-up!' The staff, however, were not going to be caught this time. They promptly ducked below the counter and fled, shutting doors behind them and shouting for help in the busy Great West Road. Hume was grabbing what notes he could and pushing them into a blue holdall when the branch manager, Mr Eric Aires, ran at him from behind a pillar. Hume flung him off and fired, wounding him severely.

After an abortive (and insanely reckless) attempt to get at the man he held responsible for doing him out of the £40,000 on the previous occasion, Hume hurried from the building, went to Kew Bridge station, and bought a ticket to Waterloo. In the lavatory he donned J. S. Bird's moustache and spectacles, transferred his haul from the blue holdall to a brown bag he had carried inside it, and hid the holdall on top of a cistern. He then caught a train, risked breaking his neck by jumping from it as it slowed down near Barnes Bridge station, and took a bus to Hammersmith. From there he went to London Airport left-luggage office, where he had deposited a suitcase with clothing and a ticket to Zurich.

It had been a tough job, resulting in only £300 profit, and the consequences were serious. Following the discovery of a raincoat he had left on the train, and helped by descriptions from the staff of the Midland Bank, the police were able to connect the robbery with Donald Brown, well-known as the alias used by Hume at the time he made his 'Confession' to the *Sunday Pictorial*. The hunt was up.

Later that autumn it appears that Hume made a third trip to Canada, returning with £1,700 which he claimed to have earned from employment with an electronics firm. A simple need for money may have been the reason for the journey, for the £300 from the Midland Bank could not have lasted long. As John Williams notes in his book, however, this last visit is shrouded in mystery, and Hume makes no mention of it in the *Sunday Pictorial* articles.

He spent his last free Christmas with Trudi and her parents, though by this time her suspicions had greatly strengthened that he was not all—or rather, was a great deal more than—he appeared to be. She had discovered a gun in his possession, a bullet, and a police reward poster which he had torn down when in London. She begged him to get rid of the gun and to tell her the truth, but he managed to put her off once again, and to trade on her affection.

He had already, in fact, decided on another exploit: a raid on the Gewerbe Bank in Zurich. Such a plan appears to have been in the back of his mind for some time. He had, however, no immediate need of cash if the story of the £1,700 was true, and one is led to wonder whether there might not have been a less conscious reason. Whether or not he admitted it to himself, he must have begun to realise that he could not for much longer keep the shaky edifice of imposture, lies and subterfuge from collapsing about him. So totally unrealistic a plan may well have been a subconscious wish to be done with it all—a final forlorn gesture of defiance against the society for which he had felt all his life such a festering hatred. He himself seemed unable to give any adequate reason for the reckless project, nor even to have felt any real confidence in its outcome.

On the morning of Friday, 30 January, having spent the previous night in the English church, he put his gun in a cardboard box he had taken from the church, and entered the Gewerbe Bank at about 11.30. He put the box on the counter and at once fired through it at one of the clerks, Walter Schenkel. In the confusion that followed, he jumped over the counter and grabbed as much money as he could. As he tried to force open the cash drawers, the wounded man managed to set off the alarm. Another clerk, Edwin Hug, struggled with Hume, but he broke away and ran out into the street. Led by Hug and a junior bank clerk named Fitze, the staff—joined by passers-by—pursued him down the Rami-strasse as he tried to reach a network of alleyways near the river. He turned several times and tried to fire at the crowd, but his pistol jammed. Running on, he fled into a small square where there was a cab rank. One of the drivers, fifty-year-old Arthur Maag, hearing the shouts and quickly grasp-ing what was happening, dived at him. Hume fired, and Maag fell mortally wounded. Almost at once Hume was caught and held by Gustav Angstmann, a hotel cook. The furious crowd grabbed at him, and had it not been for the speedy arrival of the police he might well have been lynched.

When first interrogated by the authorities, he said his name was John Stanislaw, shouting at them that he was a Polish civilian working for the American Air Force in Germany, and that he had arrived in Zurich from Weisbaden the previous day. After several hours, the arrival of a Polish interpreter put an end to that somewhat desperate attempt at deception, and it was only a short while before his true identity—through John Stephen Bird, John F. Lea, Johnny Bird and Donald Brown—became known.

He was kept in custody in Regensdorf prison, just outside Zurich, for nearly eight months before being brought to trial.

THE SWISS TRIAL

The trial of BRIAN DONALD HUME *for the murder of Arthur Maag, a taxi-driver, opened at Winterthur, Switzerland, on Thursday, 24 September 1959, under the Court President,* DR HANS GUT, *and before a jury of twelve members.*

A five-count indictment accused him of murder, attempted murder, armed robbery of a Zurich bank, threatening people's lives, and breaking the aliens regulations. In the course of the trial, HUME *said that he accepted the case for the Prosecution.*

The proceedings began with the interrogation of HUME *by* THE PRESIDENT, *the replies being translated by the Court interpreter,* DR WACH.

Asked if he was married and had a child, HUME *replied:* 'Yes, but it was not mine. The father was Stanley Setty.'*

THE PRESIDENT: Where is Mr Stanley Setty?—He is not around any more.

Asked how Setty died, HUME *said by violence, and added that he was willing to give the facts if he was not to be tried for that murder again. He fought Setty with a knife out of jealousy. When* THE PRESIDENT *pointed out to him that he had previously claimed that the quarrel was on account of the fact that Setty kicked his dog,* HUME *replied that he had given both stories.*

THE PRESIDENT: Is it true that after the death of Setty you stole things?

---

*Mr David Jacobs, of M. A. Jacobs & Sons, solicitors, London, issued a statement the same night: 'I have been asked by Mrs Cynthia Webb, formerly the wife of Mr Brian Donald Hume, who is at present on trial for murder in Switzerland, to say that the statement alleged to have been made by Hume during the course of his trial to the effect that Setty is the father of his child is completely untrue, and that Mrs Hume, as she then was, gave evidence at the Central Criminal Court, when in 1950 Hume was on trial for the murder of Stanley Setty, that she had never met Setty in her life. In 1951 Mrs Webb's marriage with Hume was dissolved on the ground of her husband's cruelty, and he is the father of her child.'

THE DEFENDANT: Yes. A lot of money. Ninety per cent of it was also smothered in blood as a result of the fight. There was a little money that was not smothered in blood. That I used. It is a fact that Scotland Yard only found two or three of the two hundred £5 notes in Setty's pocket. Only two of them could be used. The others were partly smothered in blood and damaged by a knife and could not be used. The fight took place all over the room, and in several rooms there was blood everywhere—on the furniture and on the floor. I sent one carpet to be dyed, but the police found bloodstains on the floor and carpets. I sawed off Setty's head and legs, and the parcels were thrown from an aircraft.

At one point during the examination, HUME *said to the interpreter:* 'You tell him [the President] that if it comes to a slanging match, I will rip him to bits physically. (*This remark, it appears, was not translated by the interpreter.*)

THE PRESIDENT: You obtained a second passport under the name of Stephen Bird?—If you think so, it will be so.

THE PRESIDENT: You only make yourself ridiculous by such answers.

Questioned further on the matter of the passports, HUME *made no reply.*

THE PRESIDENT: As long as I have been in this criminal court, you are the first person to refuse answers. It will not work in your favour.

THE DEPFENDANT (*to the interpreter*): Tell him to get lost.

The interpreter looked puzzled, and HUME *repeated the words.* THE PRESIDENT *continued his questions but* HUME *still refused to answer for some minutes.*

THE PRESIDENT: Why did you need the pistol?—I felt lonely.

THE PRESIDENT *asked if it was correct that Hume attacked a bank in August 1958. At first* HUME *did not reply, then, after consultation with his lawyer, said that he had robbed the Midland Bank in Brentford; he added that he had spent two or three weeks in London preparing and planning the robbery.*

THE PRESIDENT: Did you plan this bank robbery like a military operation?—Yes.

How did you carry out this robbery?—I went through the

door and held up the cashier with the pistol. I had been reconnoitring, and returned just before closing time. I went in and held up the clerk.

How did he react?—He didn't react quickly.

What did you do then?—The clerk thought it was a joke. I showed him I was not kidding. I shot.

Did he fall down?—Yes.

What happened then?—I went through and held up the three other clerks.

What did they do?—I robbed the Midland Bank. I got about £1,500 sterling. I plead guilty. Is this sufficient for the jury?

THE PRESIDENT *asked whether Miss Trudi Sommer knew where the money came from, and whether she agreed that it should be hidden under a mattress.* HUME *replied that of course she did not know: nobody knew anything about the bank raid except himself. He agreed that he arrived in Zurich on 3 August and stayed there for a short time. Asked if he made any trips with Trudi Sommer, he replied that he might have done. Then he shouted*: 'I know you are trying to crucify me. I have admitted doing the raid. The President knows that I have insulted a friend of his, Dr Horwaths [*a senior police official in Zurich*]. He is trying to crucify me under the old pals act.'

THE INTERPRETER: I don't think so.

THE PRESIDENT: What was the reason for your trips to East Germany?—I was in prison with Dr Klaus Fuchs, and he gave me a message to take to his father in Eastern Germany, but the principal reason for my trips to the East was to compare Communist countries and the West.

THE PRESIDENT: Did you also work as a spy?—I took some photographs of the United States military airport in Maine, United States, and took them to Eastern Germany and delivered them to the East German Government.

HUME *admitted that he possessed three automatic pistols. Two of these had been taken by the police and the third was still hidden behind the window of the Stadthof Hotel in Zurich, together with his passport under the name of Brown. He said that he went back to London and robbed the bank a second time purely for revenge; he was surprised by the manager, who jumped on him as he ran out*: 'We fought for a while, and then I fired. I did not know how badly he was hurt, but when I went to Canada I found out from the news-papers that he was in a serious condition.'

HUME *then told of the visit to Canada during which he worked for an electronics firm and passed a security screening. After returning to Switzerland with about £1,700, he decided to attempt a bank robbery in Zurich. This idea was quite spontaneous. About his activities in England he said*: 'I must be honest and say that I have no regrets over what happened in England; I didn't give a damn about what happened over there. I did have a conscience, as the judge is undoubtedly aware, over the Swiss raid. I couldn't reconcile myself to doing it. I was going to do it several times but it fell through.'

On the second day of the trial, Friday, 25 September, HUME's demeanour was markedly quieter and more subdued. The proceedings opened with the continuation of his inter-rogation.

Referring back to the last Canadian trip, HUME said that he returned to Europe out of affection for Trudi Sommer, although he knew that it was dangerous and that a reward was being offered by the Metropolitan Police. He thanked the President for the assurance that it did not appear to be necessary to call her as a witness. He agreed that shortly before the bank raid he became low-spirited, told Trudi Sommer that he was a bad lot and that he wanted to commit suicide. He did not tell her about the bank raids but made out that he was a spy, and said that it would be better for her not to marry him. He said that she insisted that they should get married. She took away the pistol, but later returned it to him. In Zurich he spent most of his time feeding ducks on a lake. He did not look for a hotel room but went to the English church and took away a key, returning to spend the night there. He did not sleep.

THE PRESIDENT: Why did you go into the English church? —It's very difficult to say what is going on inside one at such moments. Maybe it was the influence of Trudi Sommer. I was thinking about if there was really something about religion. I was thinking that you cannot enter paradise with a gun in your hand. I stayed all night in the church, shaving in the padré's room, eating the Communion bread and drinking the wine. I took the cardboard box from the church in which I afterwards concealed the pistol in the bank robbery.

HUME *said at first that he did not fire the gun from inside the box but took it out, pointed it, and said 'Hands up!'* He *said he could easily have shot two bank clerks if he had gone in to start blasting and shooting*: 'I am a very good shot with a pistol and have shot apples in two at twenty-five yards.'

Later THE PRESIDENT *asked*: Is it right that you put the cardboard box on the counter and shot through it?

THE DEFENDANT: Yes. Afterwards, it's easy to realise that the man could have been killed, but at the moment I just shot without thinking.

THE PRESIDENT: You have already told us that the manager of the Brentford branch of the Midland Bank was badly injured. So you had to take into account the possibility of killing?—Yes, but regarding the English bank manager, I must say that he jumped on me and threw me to the floor. He was the one who attacked me. I think he got what he was out for. I didn't have the pistol just for shooting around, but for necessity.

Describing his flight from the Gewerbe Bank, HUME *said:* That young fellow, Fitze *(a bank apprentice, aged sixteen),* deserves any reward to come from the Midland Bank. He followed me all the way. The others only joined in afterwards.

THE PRESIDENT *informed the Court that Hume had told the police that he did not shoot at Fitze because his hair was the same colour as Trudi Sommer's.*

THE PRESIDENT: What happened inside the bank?—I jumped over here *(indicating the counter on a plan of the bank),* and went into the room. The man I shot was on the ground. The other held his head in his hands. I went to the safe, and a man stood up. I thought he wanted to give the alarm so I hit him on the head with my pistol. We fought, and I hit him with my head. I didn't want to liquidate him, just to get him out of the way.

THE PRESIDENT *(referring to a remark by Hume that he knew the venture must fail)*: Why did you do it anyway?—

It's difficult to say. I didn't want my conscience to brand me as a coward.

Did your conscience not remind you that persons might be killed or wounded by shooting, even though you did not believe yourself in your success?—I didn't think it would be absolutely necessary to shoot anyone.

HUME *said that he shot the taxi-driver as he saw him running to intercept him. He was then attacked by the crowd.* I suppose a man in my position must expect that sort of thing. There was a man who pulled my hair . . . I was pretty glad when the police arrived.

Prosecution witnesses were then called.

WALTER SCHENKEL, 25, *the wounded bank cashier*: When Hume entered the bank he did not say anything and I did not see any pistol. There was an overcoat on the counter. I myself was directly behind the counter. The man then shot me. I fell down but managed to set off the alarm system. Hume then fought with another clerk, Edwin Hug. He tried to open a drawer but appeared too nervous to do so. Then he pocketed some money, jumped over the counter and ran off.

EDWIN HUG, *bank clerk, said that he was telephoning his wife when the shot was fired. He kicked a wastepaper basket between Hume's knees, then a struggle ensued, during which he was slightly hurt.*

MRS HUG *said that she was very upset and rang back ten minutes later.*

HUME: Does she love her husband? Why didn't she call back for ten minutes if she was so upset?

On the third day of the trial, further witnesses described the raid.

A Zurich ballistics expert said that bullets from a pistol which Hume was alleged to have used to shoot the taxidriver had been sent to Scotland Yard for comparison with those found after the hold-up of the Brentford branch of the Midland Bank.

The chief event of the fourth day, Tuesday, 29 September, was the presentation of a lengthy report by the Prosecution's psychiatric expert, DR GUGGENBUHL-CRAIG, *who had examined Hume in prison and found him to be sane at the time of the alleged crime. In part, the report ran:*

It is not true to say that Donald Brown was not capable at the time of his act—through insanity, imbecility or severe mental disturbance—of recognising the wrong of his deed. He was not affected at the time in his mental health or in his consciousness, nor was he mentally retarded in such a way that his capability of recognising the wrong of his deed was impaired. I could find no damage of his mental functions. He showed above-average intelligence, and his memory was good. He had no hallucinations or mad ideas.

During the whole examination he only showed deeper emotion when he talked about acts of violence. If he started to talk about these acts his face took on an expression that was so evil I often had shivers down my spine.

DR GUGGENBUHL-CRAIG *said that Hume was over-sexed but incapable of loving anyone, even his former Swiss fiancée, Trudi Sommer:* *

Donald Brown showed a complete lack of any positive feeling towards his fellow human beings. He is incapable of love. He can only hate. The hatred has nothing to do with the person subjected to it at any one moment, but is more of a general hatred towards humanity and the whole world.

Hume loved to play the part of the romantic gentleman-criminal. In a letter to Mrs Sommer written from prison in April he had said:

You will indeed hear a lot about the life I have led. I was pretty wild, much wilder than I think, but I have never done anything to hurt you or said an angry word to you. I sacrificed my freedom when you telephoned me that I should come back 10,000 kilometres from Canada to Switzerland with . . . all the police of Europe after me. There are not many men who would have done that for you, Trudi. I knew that if the English bank manager I shot at had died

*According to Victor Sims, this remark infuriated Hume. 'I may be more over-sexed than some of the Swiss,' he said, 'but I treated Trudi better than any of them. I'll always love Trudi'.

they would have hanged me. In coming back I've risked for you not only my freedom but my life.

DR GUGGENBUHL-CRAIG *explained the letter as follows*:

That this letter and the pose of the romantic outlaw is not genuine is shown in that he often quarrelled with Trudi Sommer; and he told me that he had really come back because of certain espionage opportunities. He did not want to play the part of Trudi Sommer's romantic lover, but that of a gentleman-criminal and an international master spy. This explains the discrepancy in his statement.

Hume was very vain and during the whole of the examination it was very easy to flatter him. If this 'toughness' was admired, he would always launch into long dissertations about his acts of violence.

Because he is so good at playing his various parts, he really knows the value of such qualities as friendship, love, honour, respect for other human beings, and respect of life and property. He is only really and truly himself in the part of a criminal.

DR GUGGENBUHL-CRAIG *said that he found it impossible to tell whether Hume's symptoms were the result of his past illnesses, such as the spinal cerebral meningitis from which he had suffered while with the RAF or from hereditary traits.*

When I first saw him I was surprised. He did not in any way give the impression of being ruthless. Dressed with a casual elegance, he was very polite and respectful. Right at the start he told me that he was against psychiatric investigation, as he considered himself completely responsible for his actions, and wanted to be judged as such. When he first saw me he watched me very carefully and said he was completely harmless. He described his life as a chain of misfortunes, disappointments and bad luck, which had transformed him into an embittered man. However, his real character came out when he was tranferred from a prison in Zurich to Regensdorf. He resisted this transfer with the most brutal force. When he got to Regensdorf he refused to see anyone.

The trial was concluded on the fifth day, Wednesday, 30 September. Despite HUME's *plea of Guilty, the jury were out for nearly three hours.*

THE PRESIDENT: The Court, on the verdict of the jury, finds the accused guilty first of murder, secondly of attempted murder, thirdly of robbery, fourthly of repeatedly threatening, and fifthly of offences against the Swiss federal laws concerning sojourn and residence.

A plea by his Defence counsel that he should be put in a medical care institution was rejected.

HUME *was then sentenced to imprisonment with hard labour for life. The Court also decided that should he eventually receive a remission of sentence and be released, he should be barred for another fifteen years from Swiss soil.* HUME *refused to say anything on his own behalf. As he was being taken away, he suddenly ran down the stairs from the Courthouse, dragging the guards with him. Outside, he kicked at a photographer and had to be practically thrown into the van that was waiting to take him to Regensdorf prison.*

POSTSCRIPT

Despite so much that now would seem to be clear and incontrovertible in the case of Brian Donald Hume, there is still a mist of uncertainty, of unsatisfied curiosity, that shrouds certain aspects of it, and will probably never be wholly dissipated.

There are, for instance, the discrepancies between Hume's 'Confession' and the evidence at the Old Bailey trial. Many of them, of course, are minor and understandable after the lapse of time between the events, but one or two are of greater interest.

The first concerns the knife which the Prosecution alleged Hume used to cut up Setty's body, after taking it to Mr Edwards, the garage mechanic, to be sharpened for that purpose. Hume himself said in his 'Confession' that the implements involved were a hacksaw and a lino knife. He considered that Mr Edwards was seriously mistaken in dating the carving-knife incident to 5 October. According to John Williams, Hume explained the matter as follows:

Many people believe that I used a carving-knife that had been newly sharpened for the whole ghastly business. Here is the truth about that carving-knife. Some weeks previously I had arrived back, late for dinner. I had some horseflesh—hard to get then—for my dog. My wife was cross, but even more upset when I borrowed her best carver to cut up the flesh for the dog. When she insisted that she would not have her best knife used for slicing up horsemeat I retaliated: 'Right, you'll wait for me a little longer.' Then, even though my meal was getting cold, I took another carver, an old one, down to the garage to have it sharpened. But that carver was not used [for Setty's dismemberment].

If Hume's story is true, this is a confusion of dates which

could have been vitally important. Harder to reconcile is the divergence between Hume's statement in the 'Confession' that he left 620B Finchley Road before Mrs Stride arrived on the afternoon on the 5th, and the detailed evidence she herself gave of his presence there: the floor-cloth, the missing carpet, the instructions that he was not to be disturbed in the kitchen—evidence he himself to some extent followed at the trial.

Then there is the evidence of Godfrey Marsh, the car-hire chauffeur, that, when he drove Hume to Elstree on the morning of the 6th (to recover the car left there the previous afternoon), Hume transferred two parcels to a Singer car; 'one was oblong and looked like a carpet tied at the ends and in the middle with string. The other was smaller and covered with brown paper.'

The two parcels containing the head and the other parts of Setty's body had, of course, been dropped into the sea the previous day (5 October). The third parcel was waiting in the flat for Hume to take down to his car, helped by the painter, on his return from Elstree later on the 6th. Neither in Hume's first statement, nor in his 'Confession', is there any mention of these extra parcels, and, according to John Williams, he was bewildered by what he heard. It is possible that there was some confusion between the parcels and the dog. The fact that Tony went with Hume to Elstree on the 5th and was left in the car to be picked up the next morning does not appear until the 'Confession'. Mr Marsh's evidence, however, is extraordinarily detailed, and the whole thing remains a mystery.

Most interesting of all is the fact that on the 4th Hume was apparently able to attack Setty, struggle with him, stab him to death, then drag his body across several rooms in the flat and clear up the mess (including a broken lamp-stand) unheard by anyone in the building. Mrs Hume's evidence in this respect was unchallenged, and it was completely borne out by the evidence of Mr Spencer, who lived in the flat directly below and was at home during the time. While admitting that the rooms in the flats were not situated exactly one above the other, he was quite certain that if anything unusual had taken place he would have heard it. No shadow of doubt was ever cast on either of these two pieces of evidence.*

In July 1974 Dame Rebecca West, who covered Hume's trial at the Old Bailey, wrote: † 'I do not think anybody will ever discover the truth about the Setty–Hume case now.'

In fact, Dame Rebecca remains firmly convinced that Hume was not the murderer of Stanley Setty:

> My impression was that though Hume was a horror—an infantile, grouchy, grumbling, envying horror—he had not got to the point of murder then, though he was to come to it. I think he was inspired by the trial and imprisonment.
>
> Of course, I knew that Hume had confessed to the murder of Setty before my essay was published in *A Train of Powder*. He started confessing very soon after he got into prison, and continued to produce confessions at intervals for years, but I think there was definite reason not to take them seriously, as I learned on good authority. They always showed ignorance of a detail known to the police which had never been published.
>
> I made most careful inquiries into the confessions, and it is my firm belief that they mean nothing.

Ex-Detective Superintendent Colin MacDougall, on the other hand, has no doubt as to his guilt, and is convinced that there was no secret evidence which was not brought out

*Yet another minor mystery was mentioned to me recently by His Honour Judge Elam, who was Junior Treasury Counsel at the time of Hume's trial at the Old Bailey. The names of Setty and Hume, he said, had been blazoned across the press of the entire country for weeks before and during the trial. Mr Justice Sellers started his summing-up on Wednesday, 25 January 1950, but was unable to conclude it that afternoon. During the evening the Prosecution received a telephone call. The caller—who surely must hold the record for keeping out of other people's affairs—said he understood there was some case going on concerning a man called Hume, who was supposed to have dropped some parcels into the sea tied up with rope. 'I don't know if it's of any interest,' the caller continued, 'but just around that time Hume bought the rope, or some rope, from our shop.' When asked where the shop was, the caller replied, 'Oh, just across the road from Hume's flat.' By the time this potentially important piece of information was received it was too late for it to be put in evidence.

I. B.

†In a letter to the author.

during the trial. As regards Mac, Greenie and The Boy, he says: * 'I myself, and the other two police officers, were perfectly aware at the time that Hume was basing his descriptions of the three imaginary men on ourselves.' He considers that, apart from a few natural inconsistencies regarding timing and other minor details, the 'Confession' coincided with the facts as gathered by the police, and was—as far as Hume could remember it—the truth.

Asked his personal view of Hume, Superintendent Mac-Dougall replied: 'I should say he was at times almost un-balanced, but sane in the legal sense. He had a violent temper, though he was not abusive to the police. Incidentally, he had no idea at all of aeroplane navigation.'

When sentencing Hume to life imprisonment in Switzer-land, the President of the Court said to him: 'Persons sentenced bear their imprisonment better if they take it with a certain amount of good-will and cheerfulness, and the burden is less heavy to bear if one feels the punishment is just. You will find the punishment harder to bear if you oppose it inside yourself.'

At first, according to John Williams, it seemed that Hume was taking the President's words to heart. He began his term in Regensdorf with three months' solitary confinement, and his behaviour during that period was sufficiently co-operative to earn him a week's remission. He was permitted to receive parcels from Trudi Sommer; when his spell of solitary confine-ment was over and he was allowed one visitor, it was Trudi he asked to see. Later he was allowed books and a typewriter in his cell, where he wrote stories and articles.

As time went on, however, he became increasingly violent and recalcitrant. He misbehaved in petty, vicious ways, such as breaking windows and throwing pebbles at the priest during church services. He spent his days confined to his cell making envelopes, and during exercise periods three warders had to be assigned to keeping him in order. He talked about making preparations for a bid to escape, and when his plan

*In conversation with the author. Colin MacDougall retired in 1966 with the rank of Deputy Commander, after nearly forty-one years in the police force.

was scotched before it could even get started (if indeed it was ever seriously meant), his violence increased to physical attacks on the guards, and acts of destruction.

Mr F. Donal Barry, CBE, who was Senior Legal Assistant with the Director of Public Prosecutions at the time of Hume's trial, refers* to Regensdorf as

> a very severe prison indeed, inaccessibly situated on the top of a mountain and quite impossible to escape from. Most of the very few letters which Hume was allowed to write were addressed to the DPP and other authorities, asking us if we would extradite him to stand trial for attempted murder on the Great West Road (the Midland Bank robbery). We were, however, very reluctant to do so because our case against him was not a strong one, and in any event he was safely incarcerated elsewhere. The Swiss authorities also asked us to take him—because he was such a damned nuisance—but we refused: we were no keener to have him on our hands than they were. He was a very unpleasant man.

*In a conversation with the author.